The Essential James Luther Adams

The Essential
James Luther Adams
Selected Essays and Addresses

Edited and introduced by
George Kimmich Beach

Skinner House Books
Boston

Published by Skinner House Books. Skinner House Books is an imprint of the Unitarian Universalist Association of Congregations, a liberal religious organization with more than 1,000 congregations in the U.S. and Canada. 25 Beacon Street, Boston, MA 02108-2800.

Printed in the USA.

ISBN 1-55896-352-9
978-1-55896-352-8

10 9 8 7 6 5 4
08 07 06

Acknowledgments
"The Evolution of My Social Concern" was originally published in *The Unitarian Universalist Christian* 32, nos. 1 & 2 (1977):12–24. Reprinted by permission of *The Unitarian Universalist Christian*, the journal of the Unitarian Universalist Christian Fellowship.

"Theological Bases of Social Action" was originally published as "Theological Bases of Social Action" by James Luther Adams, *The Journal of Religious Thought* 8, no. 1 (autumn/winter, 1950-51): 6-21. Reprinted by permission.

"Neither Mere Morality Nor Mere God" and "The Prophetic Covenant and Social Concern" are from *An Examined Faith* by James Luther Adams, edited by George K. Beach. © 1991 by George K. Beach. Reprinted by permission of Beacon Press, Boston.

To my father,
Stephen Holbrook Beach

Your voice lifted,
singing out in the great congregation
without a trace of self-consciousness.

Contents

Introduction

"The violin that I carried as a child when I made the rounds with my preacher-father was important to me in Chicago. The insistence on discipline enables one to think and enrich the memory and ultimately to achieve self-identity, so I managed to secure a violin teacher, a first violinist in the Chicago Symphony Orchestra. I told him I wanted to play Mozart and Handel as soon as possible. He took me on. Finally one Sunday morning after I had played a section of a Handel sonata for him, I said in despair, "I know that was a rotten job. Yet I have practiced two hours every day!" Whereupon this musician of high integrity said patiently, "Mr. Adams, what matters is not the amount of time you spend practicing. What matters is the quality of intelligence you apply to the bow." It was not long before I let him off the hook by discontinuing my lessons."

—James Luther Adams, *Not Without Dust and Heat*

What manner of man was James Luther Adams? His story of taking up the violin in middle-age provides several clues. He was an over-achiever, conscious of the fact and able to smile at himself for it, and confident that self-discipline is the engine of an enlarged humanity.

At the time this story occurred, Adams was a professor of religious social ethics at Meadville Theological School, the Unitarian seminary in Chicago. He was also a social activist engaged in issues of racism, civil liberties, and politics throughout the city. Somehow, he still found time to practice the violin. Yes, but two hours a day? Hyperbole is a raconteur's best friend, and as one might guess from this story, Adams was an incurable storyteller.

He was also an incurable self-improver. Practicing the violin served to "enrich the memory and ultimately to achieve self-identity." The importance of personal discipline in developing a well-focused sense of self is a recurrent theme in Adams's reflections. He saw his life story as the quest to fulfill his vocation, in the fundamental sense a calling to the tasks of one's true humanity. No wonder John Milton's epithet for God, "the Great Taskmaster," often sprang to his mind.

The story of his taking up the violin in adulthood also reflects his love for music. Adams speaks of music as "a means of grace," a creative reality that transcends reason and enables new understandings of life to emerge. In his mid-life autobiographical essay, "Taking Time Seriously," he describes how singing Bach's *Mass in B minor* with a large chorus became a pivotal experience in his spiritual life and vocation. The experience moved him to ask: What will *I* contribute to the living tradition of faith so richly augmented by Bach? God, for Adams, is experienced at those points where our creative energies are evoked and our lives are given impetus and direction.

Taking up the violin also reflects the dominant role his father played in his childhood experience. In his autobiography, Adams speaks candidly of growing up as the son of a fundamentalist minister and of seeing his father as "the image of God"—an entirely righteous, unbending, punishing God. From this father the young Adams sought (and ultimately seems to have found) signs of love and mercy. As difficult as his relationship with his father must have been, he continued to hold his father in deep respect, even awe. He calls him "a man of principle," a man willing to take a stand for his beliefs even at great personal cost.

Adams's father demonstrated what was to become basic in Adams's thought, the development of criteria by which to judge culture and religion. Adams developed his sense of the importance of "standards" through his study of comparative literature at Harvard College under Professor Irving Babbitt, who became his intellectual father. Best known for his "literary humanism," Babbitt's assertion of "the primacy of the will" became a key concept in Adams's critique of liberalism.

During his undergraduate years, Adams overthrew the fundamentalist faith he had adopted from his parents. He recognized its radically world-negating tendency, leading the believer almost to relish the thought of an apocalyptic end of the world. Nevertheless, Adams was aware of retaining a basic perspective on time and history from his childhood faith, namely an eschatological sense of time and history. In his thought, history is directed to a goal; time is an eternally present moment of decision. Either life is a life of commitment, or else it is a meaningless pastime.

These basic concerns did not disappear when he became a Unitarian. Adams asked himself: What transcendent purpose and goal will give meaning to my life? He answered: Commitment to the community of justice and love under the grace and guidance of God, the Great Taskmaster. Adams's most succinct definition of God was "the community-forming power."

For Adams, the genius of a liberal faith is that it is self-critical and, therefore, open to—even demanding of—self-reform. He memorably paraphrased Socrates, "An unexamined faith is not worth having." No wonder, then, that Adams should become one of the sharpest critics of religious liberalism, with its characteristic "once-born" stance, an outlook that sees no need for spiritual transformation. Insofar as they are uncommitted, Adams said, religious liberals are self-frustrating.

Yet Adams's sharpest criticisms went down more easily, thanks to his underlying optimism and capacity for self-satire. One of his most felicitous epithets is "the smiling prophet." He took himself seriously but always escaped taking himself *too* seriously. In his story about taking up the violin, we see a man with a robust ego who always manages to avoid egotism: "He took me on"—the one who wanted to be playing Mozart and Handel "as soon as possible"!

James Luther Adams conveys meaning through story-telling. His violin story is a parable; it tells "what life is like." We may say, then: What counts in life is not how much time you spend laboring to "get it right," but rather the intelligence you apply to the task. Without the bow, the body of the violin, however finely made, can make no music. Adams would have us press our very lives against the body of our existence, as a musician presses the bow against the violin, but "do it with intelligence." Likewise, he would have us be persons of faith, but of an examined—self-critical and prophetically intentional—faith.

In his autobiography Adams lets the story of his violin lesson speak for itself. It is like a prism that breaks the light into several hues. It sparkles with meaning. It reflects both a strong personality and strong ideas. These contrasting elements, the personal and the conceptual, are evident throughout the essays gathered in this volume. Their interweaving is the enduring stuff of the man and his mind, the essential James Luther Adams.

James Luther Adams was born in Ritzville, Washington, in 1901, the son of an itinerant Baptist minister and farmer. His father, James Carey Adams, converted to the

Plymouth Brethren church and became, after the example of St. Paul, a "tentmaker": he would accept no pay for preaching the Gospel; thereafter he earned his living from farming. Adams's mother, Lella Mae Bartlett, was likewise a "true believer."

Still a young boy when his father's health failed, young Luther (as the family addressed him) worked at numerous jobs to help support his parents and two sisters. As a teenager he learned shorthand and rose, in a few years' time, to the lucrative position of secretary to a superintendent on the Northern Pacific Railroad. Reflecting on this phase of Adams's early life, Max Stackhouse believes Adams might have become a railroad tycoon! But as Adams himself tells the story, "I just wanted to learn something about Shakespeare." He entered the University of Minnesota in 1920 and continued to work nights in the railroad yards.

In Minneapolis Adams encountered two powerful Unitarians, the Reverend John Dietrich, the outspoken humanist minister of the Unitarian Society, and Professor Frank Rarig, a renowned teacher of rhetoric at the university. After considering a career in law, Adams decided to go with his bent—or his calling; he entered Harvard Divinity School, on his way to becoming a Unitarian minister. After graduating he served as minister in two Unitarian congregations, in Salem and Wellesley Hills, Massachusetts. In Salem he met Margaret Ann Young, a pianist recently graduated from the New England Conservatory. They married and raised three daughters, Eloise, Elaine, and Barbara. Some years later, in Chicago, Margaret became a professional social worker with strong personal commitments to racial and economic justice. Margaret would sometimes goad Adams into activism. He said, "Margaret always insisted on putting her towel to *the left* of mine in the bathroom. She was the truly radical one in the family."

While he was serving as a parish minister during the 1920s and 1930s, Adams pursued graduate studies in comparative literature at Harvard University under professors Irving Babbitt and George Lyman Kittredge. Subsequently he taught English literature at Boston University. During this period he sought to "complete his education" through travel and study in England, France, and Germany. A few years later, in anticipation of his appointment to teach religious social ethics at Meadville Theological School, he undertook a final, extended sojourn in Germany. Rudolf Otto, the famous Marburg University scholar of comparative religions, became his close friend. Adams's discussions with many theologians and church leaders in Germany—some collaborated with the Nazis, others resisted, and most remained silent—became pivotal experiences in his life. The rise of Nazism signified to Adams an epochal crisis for liberal democracy, a crisis to which religious communities were ill-prepared to respond.

In Chicago, and in later years in Cambridge, Massachusetts, the Adams home became a weekly gathering place for generations of theological students. Adams also became active in numerous political and social causes. The Independent Voters of Illinois (IVI), which he helped found and lead, grew to become a powerful reform organization in Chicago politics. His political experiences with the IVI, the American Civil Liberties Union, and other liberal, activist associations underlie his extensive writings on the role of voluntary associations in a democratic society.

Adams was active in church life throughout his career. The ministry always lay at the heart of his sense of vocation. He was instrumental in founding the Greenfield Group in New England, and later, the Prairie Group in the Midwest, associations through which ministers maintained intellectual and spiritual disciplines. Confronting the organizational and intellectual lethargy into which Unitarianism had drifted during the 1930s, Adams became a leader in the movement to revitalize the American Unitarian Association through a powerful Commission of Appraisal. With renewed growth and bold new programs for religious education, publications, church extension, international service, and youth work, this effort bore fruit in the 1940s and 1950s, ultimately leading to the creation of the Unitarian Universalist Association in 1961. My own first encounter with Adams at a continental conference of Unitarian Universalist youth in Indiana is characteristic of the way he touched countless lives beyond the university. I remember his speaking of J. D. Salinger's *The Catcher in the Rye* as a major document of the time, reflecting the spiritual confusion and longing of our "silent generation." Adams believed that youth movements were key to historical change, and he wanted to keep in touch with what young people were thinking. Opening himself to others, he made himself accessible to them.

Adams had been drawn to the work of Paul Tillich before the distinguished, radical theologian came to the United States as a refugee from Nazi Germany. Afterward, he became a major interpreter of Tillich's thought. Adams translated and in 1948 secured the publication of *The Protestant Era,* Tillich's theological interpretations of contemporary history and society. Thus Tillich redirected theological thought from "churchly" to political and cultural concerns. Adams's first book, *Paul Tillich's Philosophy of Culture, Science, and Religion*, based on his 1945 doctoral dissertation at the University of Chicago Divinity School, reflects this shift. In Tillich's existentialism Adams found the philosophical basis for a renewed liberal faith; and in his religious socialism he found the expression of a prophetic social ethic. Tillich did not retreat from the crisis of the age; he "took time seriously."

When Adams returned to Harvard University to become professor of Christian social ethics on the Divinity School faculty in 1956, Paul Tillich—a campus luminary—became his faculty colleague. In Cambridge Jim and Margaret's home again became a center for weekly late-evening conversations with Unitarian students. Adams would hold forth on everything from the music of Anton Webern to the role of memorial services in the grieving process; we students would vent our frustrations with the reigning Barthian neo-orthodoxy, or with the "irrelevance" of our courses to "real ministry."

Thus Jim and Margaret created a small, caring community. For me as a young theological student, it was the model of an intentional community within the church universal. The two must remain in dialectical relation and tension, Adams would insist, but his passion was for the small group, the *ecclisiola in ecclesia*. He often spoke of how small groups nurture and sustain individual development and effect renewal within large communities. "By their groups you shall know them!"

After he reached Harvard's mandatory retirement age of sixty-five, Adams—hardly ready to retire—accepted an appointment to teach at Andover Newton Theological School in Newton, Massachusetts. Subsequently he received yet another temporary appointment, to Meadville/Lombard Theological School; once again he and Margaret moved to Chicago. In 1976, Beacon Press published a second volume of his essays, *On Being Human Religiously*, edited and introduced by his former student, Max Stackhouse. Not long after their final return to Cambridge in 1978, Margaret, Jim's beloved wife of fifty years, succumbed to cancer.

Jim's final years were remarkably productive. Three volumes of his essays, written over several decades, were published: *Voluntary Associations*, edited by J. Ronald Engel, and *The Prophethood of All Believers* and *An Ex-*

amined Faith, which I edited and introduced. I consulted with him extensively while preparing the books I edited for publication; Adams approved the selections and the edited manuscripts, including revisions to earlier works to include nonsexist terms. Why he did not himself gather his writings into books, but entrusted the process to former students, is difficult to say; he never volunteered to explain it, and it felt impertinent to ask. I think he was simply too busy with the next project to look back. "Whoever puts his hand to the plow and looks back is not fit for the kingdom of God" (Luke 9:62). Through these publications, Adams's widely scattered writings have been made available to a larger audience.

During the last years of his life, Adams continued to entertain a daily stream of visitors and to maintain his voluminous correspondence with friends, former students, and academic colleagues. Colleagues and friends in Boston formed the James Luther Adams Foundation and undertook two major projects. They transformed Adams's priceless 8 mm. films from Germany in the 1930s—silent images of church and university figures and of political demonstrations—into videotapes, with new commentaries by Adams and his colleague, George H. Williams.

The Foundation also provided assistants—first Linda Barnes and later Louise Des Marais—to transcribe and edit his autobiography. It ran to some 1,400 pages in the original typescript and had to be cut almost in half for publication. The book appeared shortly after his death, titled *Not Without Dust and Heat*, a phrase from John Milton's classic essay, "Areopagitica."

> I cannot praise a fugitive and cloister'd virtue, unexercis'd and unbreath'd, that never sallies out and sees her adversary, but slinks out of the race, where that immortall garland is to be run for, not without dust and heat.

Throughout his last years, Adams experienced continuous discomfort and often intense back pain due to the progressive disintegration of his vertebrae. For several years he wore a back brace; like a turtle shell it encircled his chest with a steel arm. He ultimately cast the brace off as more trouble than it was worth. On July 26, 1994, at the age of ninety-two, he died at home, in the house he and Margaret had built on the original Andrews Norton family estate, Shady Hill.

What can we learn from James Luther Adams? We can learn how to use a cluster of concepts that are basic to both theological and social-ethical thought: power, covenant, vocation, positive law and natural law, periodization of history, voluntarism and rationalism, voluntary and involuntary associations, root metaphors, law and grace, historical and mystical religion, and prophetic and sacramental faith. Paired concepts are typical of the dialectical mode of Adams's thought: tension and change mark whatever is alive, vital, and meaningful. His ideas—the basis for a revitalized liberalism in religion and politics alike—are today more timely than ever.

Adams constantly drew on his vast knowledge of history, sociology, psychology, the arts, and theology. His essays convey his distinctive viewpoint; they range widely and are often difficult to classify by subject. But then, Adams himself is difficult to classify. He was deeply influenced by two preeminent philosophical theologians of this century, Alfred North Whitehead and Paul Tillich. He also taught courses and wrote extensively about Ernst Troeltsch, the German historian, sociologist, and liberal Protestant theologian of the early decades of this century. Although he is the least well-known of the three, Troeltsch was the most closely akin to Adams in his scholarly interests and his intellectual bent. Once asked if he were "a Whiteheadian or a Tillichean," Adams replied with a wry smile, "There is always Troeltsch." He was not one to be pigeonholed.

In his historical study, *The Unitarians and the Universalists*, David Robinson comments that "Adams's spiritual odyssey incarnates much of the story of twentieth century liberal religion." Robinson cites historian George H. Williams's judgment that Adams ranks with William Ellery Channing and Henry Whitney Bellows as the three greatest American Unitarian leaders. These appraisals seem surprising insofar as the Christian theological stance at which he arrived, early in his odyssey, put

Adams at odds with the increasingly dominant scientific humanism of his adopted denomination. It is understandable only as one also sees in contemporary Unitarian Universalist circles a countervailing movement to renew questions of faith and transcendence—a movement toward a biblical humanism.

Adams helped many of us rediscover that faith is an "original decision" and a turning toward transcendence. As such it need not be a blind or a mindless faith. It can be a critically "examined faith," except that the *criteria* for its continuing evaluation and its consequent modification would be markedly different from those of rationalism or scientism.

The criteria would be reflexive and personal: through questioning we should "grow in our very questions," as Adams said. The criteria would also be ontological: questions of being go before questions of doing—"isness" precedes and shapes "oughtness" (in Friedrich von Huegel's terms, often used by Adams). And the criteria would be ethical: it is by the seriousness of our commitments to social justice that the quality of our faith is known—"By their fruits shall you know them" (Matthew 7:16). Further, serious social-ethical commitments will be borne by voluntary associations—"By their *groups* shall you know them" (Adams's variation on Jesus' saying). The theory and practice of voluntary associations in society became Adams's recurrent theme.

But none of these things explains the deep impression Adams made on countless students, colleagues, audiences, friends. What we have felt, I believe, is that in Adams we encountered one who fought for and achieved a principle of authentic faith, namely that we take seriously the demands of time and history to make a difference in the struggle for justice—under the Great Taskmaster's eye—and that we do so with loving kindness, laughter, and grace.

George Kimmich Beach
Madison, Virginia

Faith and Freedom

I call that church free which enters into covenant with the ground of freedom, that sustaining, judging, transforming power not made with hands. It protests against the idolatry of any human claim to absolute truth or authority. This covenant is the charter and joy of worship in the beauty of holiness.

I call that church free which in covenant with that divine community-forming power brings the individual, even the unacceptable, into a caring, trusting fellowship that protects and nourishes his or her integrity and spiritual freedom. Its goal is the prophethood and the priesthood of all believers—the one for the liberty of prophesying, the other for the ministry of healing. It therefore protests against the infringement of autonomy or participation, whether it be in the church, the state, the family, the daily work (or the lack of it), or in other social spheres.

I call that church free which liberates from bondage to the principalities and power of the world, whether churchly or secular, and which promotes the continuing reformation of its own and other institutions. It pro-

tests against routine conformity or thoughtless noncon-
formity that lead to deformity of mind and heart and
community.

I call that church free which in charity promotes freedom in fellowship, seeking unity in diversity. This unity
is a potential gift, sought through devotion to the transforming power of creative interchange in generous dialogue. But it will remain unity in diversity.

I call that church free which responds in responsibility to the Spirit that bloweth where it listeth. The tide
of the Spirit finds utterance ever and again through a
minority. It invites and engenders liberation from repres-
sion and exploitation, whether of nation or economic
system, of race or sex or class. It bursts through rigid,
cramping inheritance, giving rise to new language, to
new forms of cooperation, to new and broader fellowship. The church of the Spirit is a pilgrim church on
adventure.

I call that church free which is not bound to the present,
which cowers not before the vaunted spirit of the times.
It earns and creates a tradition binding together past,
present, and future in a living tether, in a continuing
covenant and identity, bringing forth treasures both new
and old. God speaks, God has also spoken.

I call that church free which is not imprisoned in itself or in a sect. In loyalty to its own historic character
and norms, it is open to insight and conscience from
every source. The church that would be free yearns to
belong to the church universal, catholic and invisible.

But the church is never wholly free: It tolerates injustice, special privilege, and indifference to suffering, as though it were not accountable to a tribunal higher than the world's. It passes by on the other side, thus breaking the covenant. In the midst of this unfreedom the congregation comes together to adore that which is holy, to confess its own brokenness, and to renew the covenant.

I call that church free which does not cringe in despair, but casting off fear is lured by the divine persuasion to respond in hope to the light that has shown and that still shines in the darkness.

—"The Church That Is Free"
James Luther Adams, 1975

A Faith for the Free

Both faith and freedom, Adams held, are inescapable. Since we are "fated to be free" and fated to put our faith in something, ours must be a critically examined and a freely chosen faith. "An unexamined faith is not worth having"; "a faith worth having is a faith worth discussing and testing." Adams outlined "three tenets of faith for the free," placing special emphasis on the centrality of religious community. This essay was originally published in 1946.—GKB

All men and women are faithful, but not all can distinguish between faiths and separate the good from the evil. Even the great, good words of ancient religion do not always draw upon a full treasury of great and good faith. The words can circulate as debased currency, a currency that can be used for illicit traffic in credulity.

The very age and the universal appeal of religion make it almost inevitable that its words shall degenerate into a debased coinage, a coinage that sometimes deceives even the elect and that repels those who would prefer moral and intellectual integrity to "piety." Every sharp ear would detect the counterfeit ring of this debased coinage of "faith," this brummagem currency of credulity. With good reason a modern prophet has said, "the beginning of all criticism is the criticism of religion."

Not only religion as ordinarily understood requires this criticism. Religion can disguise itself in protean ways. A new faith can hide behind what appears to be irreligion. The criticism of religion must include the criticism of faiths that are concealed behind seemingly irreligious words and acts.

What, then, is faith?

To many people the word signifies the acceptance of something that puts a strain on the intelligence. Accordingly, faith is to them a belief in what is not true or in what is by nature not fact but wish.

To others the word *faith* signifies the acceptance of some belief simply because a church, a tradition, a state, a party, demands it. They may recall that St. Ignatius of Loyola once said, "We should always be disposed to believe that that which appears white to us is really black, if the hierarchy of the Church so decides." With some justification, then, they hold that faith is a belief in "some nice tenets," a "dear deceit" (as archaic as those phrases suggest), which relieves one of the responsibility of thinking for oneself; it is therefore a positively dangerous thing, a form of bigotry that will brook no questioning or criticism and that dresses itself up as "the cure for modern pride" and as "humble obedience to the will of God."

But conventionally "religious" people have no monopoly on credulity. Those who reject the inherited "faith" are sometimes only the victims of a new credulity. Nothing could be more credulous than the belief that faith dies when some traditional belief dies. Our world is full to bursting with faiths, each contending for allegiance. Hitler claimed to teach again the meaning of faith. Mussolini shouted to his disciples, "Believe, follow, and act." "Fascism," he said, "before being a party is a religion." Those who were called to put down the battalions of the brown shirts and the black shirts were asked to show the faith that lies behind freedom.

So the procession of the gods passes over the stage of our world. Human history is not the struggle between religion and irreligion; it is veritably a battle of faiths; a battle of the gods who claim human allegiance.

An Unexamined Faith Is Not Worth Having

Not long ago I heard a German exile tell a story of Nazi horror. As he reached the end of his story he became mute with revulsion and indignation. How could he speak with sufficient contempt of what the Gestapo had done to his friend? Painfully he groped for words, and then, speaking with revived fear of the Gestapo officers who had committed murder in cold blood, he asked, "Are these men completely without awe? Are they completely without faith?" Immediately he answered his own question: "There is," he said, "no such thing as a man completely without faith. What a demonic faith is the faith of the Nazis!" We can readily understand what he meant. The differences among people do not lie in the fact that some have faith and others do not. *They lie only in a difference of faith.* The Gestapo put its confidence in obedience to the Führer, in obedience to the call of "blood and soil." Its victims placed their confidence in something thicker than blood, in something stronger than death or fear of death. Whether or not this particular victim used the word "faith" or any other words from religious tradition, we do not know, but it is evident that he put his confidence in something more powerful and commanding than the Gestapo. It is possible that his was a faith for the free. In any event, such a faith did rise up against the Gestapo.

Fortunately, not many of us have had the experience of confronting Gestapo agents. We have liked to believe that we did not share *their* faith, yet we have all had some part in creating or appeasing Gestapos—and we could do it again. We have also had some part in stopping the Gestapo. In fact, the spirit, if not the brutality, of the Gestapo has to be stopped in ourselves every day, and we are not always successful, either because of our impotence or because of our lack of conviction. The faith of the unfree can raise its ugly head even in a "free" country.

Recently this fact was impressed upon me in an unforgettably vivid way. During the Second World War it was at one time my task to lecture on the Nazi faith to a large group of U.S. Army officers who were preparing for service later in the occupation army in Germany. As I lectured I realized that together with a just resentment against the Nazis I was engendering in the students an orgy of self-righteousness. This self-righteousness, I decided, ought somehow to be checked. Otherwise I might succeed only in strengthening the morale of a bumptious hundred-percent "Americanism," and that was not the faith we were supposed to be fighting for. Toward the end of the lecture I recapitulated the ideas of the Nazi "faith," stressing the Nazi belief in the superiority of the Teutons and in the inferiority of other "races." I also reminded the officers of similar attitudes to be observed in America, not only among the lunatic and subversive groups but also among respectable Americans in the army of democracy. Then I asked these army officers to pose one or two questions to be answered by each man in his own conscience. First: "Is there any essential difference between your attitude toward the Negro and the Jew, and the Nazi attitude toward other 'races'—not a difference in brutality but a difference in basic philosophy?" "If there is an essential difference," I said, "then the American soldier might logically become a defender of the Four Freedoms, but if there is no essential difference between your race philosophy and that of the Nazis, a second question should be posed: 'What are you fighting for?'"

I blush when I think of some of the responses I received. I was immediately besieged with questions like these: "Do you think we should marry the 'nigger'?" "Aren't Negroes a naturally indolent and dirty race?" "Haven't you been in business, and don't you know that every Jew is a kike?" Questions like these came back to me for over an hour. I simply repeated my question again and again: "How do you distinguish between yourself and a Nazi?" Seldom have I witnessed such agony of spirit in a public place.

Many of these Americans who could not distinguish between themselves and Nazis came from "religious" homes, or they claimed to be representatives (or even leaders) of the American faith. Apparently their faith was quite different from the faith behind the Four Freedoms. On the other hand, many of them no doubt would have disclaimed possessing anything they would call faith, yet all of them, whatever their answers to these questions, spoke the faith that was in them, and for many of them it was a trust in white, gentile supremacy—faith in the blood.

Faith is by no means dead in the world. A devil's plenty of it is loose on the planet. "A man bears beliefs," said Emerson, "as a tree bears apples." He bears beliefs about himself, about his fellows, about his work and his play, about his past, about his future, about human destiny. What he loves, what he serves, what he sacrifices for, what he tolerates, what he fights against—these signify his faith. They show what he places his confidence in.

Right or wrong, our faith must needs express itself and have its consequences for woe or weal. There is no escape. We cannot escape history, whether it be the history around us, the history behind us, or the springs of history within us, for all of these are forces that make history—and we are caught in history. Down among the nerve cells and fibers, up in the brain cells as well as out in the world around us, faith is at work—or, rather, a multitude of faiths is at work.

The question concerning faith is not, Shall I be a person of faith? The proper question is, rather, Which faith is mine? or, better, Which faith should be mine? for, whether a person craves prestige, wealth, security, or amusement, whether a person lives for country, for science, for God, or for plunder, that person is demonstrating a faith, is showing that she or he puts confidence in something.

The faiths of the twentieth century have been as powerful and influential as any that have ever been. They have created its science and its atom bombs, its nationalisms and its internationalisms, its wars and its "peace," its heroisms and its despairs, its Hollywoods and its Broadways, its Wall Streets and its Main Streets, its Gestapos and its undergrounds, its democracies and its fascisms, its socialisms and its communisms, its wealth and its poverty, its securities and its insecurities, its beliefs and its unbeliefs, its questions and its answers.

We must not believe every "pious" man's religion to be what he says it is. He may go to church regularly, he may profess some denominational affiliation, he may repeat his creed regularly, but he may actually give his deepest loyalty to something quite different from these things and from what they represent. Find out what that is and you have found his religion. You will have found his god. It will be the thing he gets most excited about, the thing that most deeply concerns him. But speak against it in the pulpit or in the Pullman car, and he may forget what he calls his religion or his god and rush "religiously" to the defense of what really concerns him. What moves him now is more important than his creed or his atheism; it gives meaning and direction to his life, to his struggles, and even to his foibles.

We Are Fated to Be Free

The fact that every man and woman, whether they will it or not, must put trust in something, is no basis for any particular faith. Rather, the necessity as well as the fact shows only that we humans must *choose*. We cannot escape making a choice, nor can we escape the responsibility for the choices we make, any more than we can escape their consequences. We cannot hide behind someone else's authority or choice. Whenever we delegate a decision to someone else, or to the Bible or a church, we have made a decision. The decision is still our own, and the claim that humility dictates the decision does not make the decision any the less our own.

We cannot escape from freedom and its responsibilities. Every attempt to do so is an act of freedom, an act that must be implicitly repeated at every moment. Freedom is our fate as well as our birthright, and we cannot, even if we wish to, slide back into vegetability. Even the abuse of freedom is a use of freedom. Hence in our kind of world *every* faith is, in a certain sense, a faith of the free, whether it is a faith that takes us with the prodigal son to eat with swine, or a faith that shackles us to a political or an ecclesiastical Führer, or a faith that generates freedom. *We have no choice but to be free in the choice of our faith.*

Just because we are compelled to make a decision and a choice we are compelled to have faith in ourselves. Even those who say they cannot trust their judgments will have to do so to the extent of deciding what they can trust. Indeed, those who claim to be able to identify an infallible authority "above" themselves really claim to be themselves infallible. Such a claim as this presupposes an unwarranted (and credulous) faith in humanity.

Even the less credulous faith that acknowledges human fallibility also requires a faith in humanity. This faith may be a more modest one than that of orthodox belief in infallibility, but it holds that a more reliable object of faith can be found if people are free to learn from each other by mutual criticism, free to discard old error, free to discover new insight, free to judge, free to test. The free person's faith is not merely a faith in oneself: It is a faith in the capacity of sincere persons to find freely together that which is worthy of confidence. John Milton, the great Puritan apostle of freedom, epitomized this faith in discussion in those ringing words that are always quoted when freedom of printing and of speech seems threatened: "Who ever knew truth put to the worse in a free and open encounter?"

The free woman and the free man are not bound to accept a faith "once delivered." Indeed, they see no virtue in accepting a faith simply on the ground that it was determined before their births. In their view, consensus, not compulsion, free and open discussion, not docile obedience, should rule in matters of faith. The denial of the right and duty to discuss one's faith is tantamount to making credulity a work of piety.

The free person does not live by an unexamined faith. To do so is to worship an idol whittled out and made into a fetish. The free person believes with Socrates that the true can be separated from the false only through observation and rational discussion. In this view the faith that cannot be discussed is a form of tyranny.

An unexamined faith is not worth having, for it can be true only by accident. A faith worth having is faith worth discussing and testing. To believe that a fence of taboo should be built around some formulation is to believe that a person can become God (or his exclusive private secretary) and speak for him. No authority, including the authority of individual conviction, is rightly exempt from discussion and criticism. The faith of the free, if it is to escape the tyranny of the arbitrary, must be available to all, testable by all (and not merely by an elite), valid for all. It is something that is intelligible and justifiable.

Three Tenets of a Faith for the Free

As creatures fated to be free, as creatures who must make responsible decisions, what may we place our confidence in? What can we have faith in? What should we serve?

1. *The first tenet of the free person's faith is that our ultimate dependence for being and freedom is upon a creative power and upon processes not of our own making.* Our ultimate faith is not in ourselves. We find ourselves historical beings, beings living in nature and history, beings having freedom in nature and in history. The forms that nature and history take possess a given, fateful character, and yet they are also fraught with meaningful possibilities.

Within this framework the person finds something dependable and also many things that are not dependable. One thing that is dependable is the order of nature and of history which the sciences are able to describe with varying degrees of precision.

How long the order of nature will continue to support human life is beyond our ken. Probably our earth and our sun will one day cool off and freeze. Moreover, everyone is condemned to what we call death. Whether beyond this death there is a new life is a matter of faith, of faith that trusts the universe as we have known it. Like one of old we may say to this universe and its ruling power, "Into thy hands I commend my spirit."

Whatever the destiny of the planet or of the individual life, a sustaining meaning is discernible and commanding in the here and now. Anyone who denies this denies that there is anything worth taking seriously or even worth talking about. Every blade of grass, every work of art, every scientific endeavor, every striving for righteousness bears witness to this meaning. Indeed, every frustration or perversion of truth, beauty or goodness also bears this witness, as the shadow points round to the sun.

One way of characterizing this meaning is to say that through it God is active or is fulfilling himself in nature and history. To be sure, the word *God* is so heavily laden with unacceptable connotations that it is for many people scarcely usable without confusion. It is therefore well for us to indicate briefly what the word signifies here. In considering this definition, however, the reader should remember that among many religious liberals no formulation is definitive and mandatory. Indeed, the word *God* may in the following formulations be replaced by the phrase, "that which ultimately concerns humans," or by the phrase, "that which we should place our confidence in." Perhaps it would be well for the reader to make these substitutions.

God (or that in which we have faith) is the inescapable, commanding reality that sustains and transforms all meaningful existence. It is inescapable, for none can live without somehow coming to terms with it. It is commanding, for it provides the structure or the process through which existence is maintained and by which any meaningful achievement is realized. (Indeed, every meaning in life is related to this commanding meaning that no one can manipulate and that stands beyond every merely personal preference or whim.) It is transforming, for it breaks through any given achievement, it invades any mind or heart open to it, luring it on to richer or more relevant achievement; it is a self-surpassing reality. God is that reality which works upon us and through us and in accord with which we can achieve truth, beauty, or goodness. It is that creativity which works in nature and history, under certain conditions creating human good in human community. Where these conditions are not met, human good, as sure as the night follows the day, will be frustrated or perverted. True freedom and individual or social health will be impaired. It is only because of this reality that, in Tennyson's words,

> . . . Spirit with spirit can meet—
> Closer is He than breathing, and nearer than hands
> and feet.

The only person who is really an atheist is one who denies that there is any reality that sustains meaning and goodness in the human venture. The true atheist is one who recognizes nothing as validly commanding. It is very difficult to find this sort of atheist, perhaps impossible.

This reality that is dependable and in which we may place our confidence is not, then, merely ourselves—in it we live and move and have our being—nor is it a mere projection of human wishes; it is a working reality that every person is coerced to live with. In this sense the faith of the free is not free; the human being is not free to work without the sustaining, commanding reality. One is free only to obstruct it or to conform to the conditions it demands for growth. This reality is, then, no human contrivance; it is a reality without which no human good can be realized and without which growth or meaning is impossible. Theists and religious humanists find common ground here. They differ in defining the context in which human existence and human good are to be understood.

The free person's faith is therefore a faith in the giver of being and freedom. Human dignity derives from the fact that to be a person means to participate in the being and freedom of this reality. If we use the terms of historical Christianity, we may say the man and the woman are made in the image of this creative reality. Under its auspices they become themselves creators.

But humanity not only participates in this divinely given being and freedom. Through the abuse of freedom it also perverts and frustrates them. It distorts or petrifies the forms of creation and freedom. Hence free persons cannot properly place their confidence in their own creations; they must depend upon a transforming reality that breaks through encrusted forms of life and thought to create new forms. Free women and men put their faith in a creative reality that is re-creative.

2. *The second tenet of the free person's faith is that the commanding, sustaining, transforming reality finds its richest focus in meaningful human history, in free, cooperative effort for the common good.* In other words, this reality fulfills our life only when people stand in right relation to each other. As historical beings, they come most fully to terms with this reality in the exercise of the freedom that works for justice in the human community. Only what creates freedom in a community of justice is dependable. "Faith is the sister of justice." Only the society that gives every person the opportunity to share in the process whereby human potentiality is realizable, only the society that creates the social forms of freedom in a community of justice (where all are given their due), only the freedom that respects the divine image and dignity in each person, are dependable. As Lincoln put it, "Those who deny freedom to others deserve it not for themselves, and, under a just God, cannot long retain it."

A faith that is not the sister of justice is bound to bring people to grief. It thwarts creation, a divinely given possibility; it robs them of their birthright of freedom in an open universe; it robs the community of the spiritual richness latent in its members; it reduces the person to a beast of burden in slavish subservience to a state, a church, or a party—to a god made by human hands. That way lie the grinding rut and tyranny of the Vatican line, the Nuremberg line, and the Moscow line, different though these lines are from each other in their fear and obstruction of freedom.

To try to manipulate or domesticate the integrity of freedom is to rely upon the unreliable—an attempt that ends in reliance on arbitrary power and upon arbitrary counsels. Sooner or later the arbitrary confronts either stagnation from within or eruption both from without and from within. The stars in their courses fight against it.

This faith in the freedom that creates the just community is the faith of the Old Testament prophets. They repudiated the idea that the meaning of life is to be achieved either by exclusive devotion to ritual or by devotion to blood and soil, the idols of the tribe. The "holy" thing in life is the participation in those processes that give body and form to universal justice. Injustice brings judgment and suffering in its train. It is tolerated only at the peril of stability and meaning.

Again and again in the history of our civilization this prophetic idea of the purpose of God in history comes to a new birth. Jesus deepened and extended the idea when he proclaimed that the kingdom of God is at hand. The reign of God, the reign of the sustaining, commanding, transforming reality, is the reign of love, a love that fulfills and goes beyond justice, a love that "cares" for the fullest personal good of all. This love is not something that is ultimately created by us or that is even at our disposal. It seizes us and transforms us, bringing us into a new kind of community that provides new channels for love.

Jesus uses the figure of the seed to describe this power. The power of God is like a seed that grows of itself if we will use our freedom to meet the conditions for its growth. It is not only a principle by which life may be guided; it is also a power that transforms life. It is a power we may trust to heal the wounds of life and to create the joy of sharing and of community. This is the power the Christian calls the forgiving, redemptive power of God, a power every person may know and experience whether or not one uses these words to describe it.

Not that it demands no wounds itself. It drew Jesus up Golgotha to a cross. Thus Jesus was not only a martyr dying for his convictions, but also the incarnation of the affirmative power of love transforming life, even in death, and creating a transforming community, a fellowship of free men and women yielding to the tides of the spirit.

This commanding, sustaining, transforming power can, at least for a time, be bottled up in dead words or in frozen instructions. (The cross has been smothered in lilies.) The sustaining, transforming reality can be perverted by willful humans, abusing their freedom, into a power that up to a point supports evil—yet, if humanity could not so abuse its freedom, it would not be free.

In history and in the human heart there are, then, destructive as well as creative powers. These destructive powers are manifest in the social as well as in the individual life, though they are most subtly destructive in the social life where the individual's egotism fights under the camouflage of the "good" of the nation, the race, the church, or the class. These destructive impulses (thoroughly familiar to the psychologist if not to their victims) seem veritably to "possess" people, blinding them, inciting them to greed, damaging the holy gifts God provides. This is precisely the reason for the need of the redemptive, transforming power. Indeed "pious" folk are often the most in need of the transformation.

3. *The third tenet of the free person's faith is that the achievement of freedom in community requires the power of organization and the organization of power.* The free person will be unfree, will be a victim of tyranny from within or from without, if his or her faith does not assume *form*, in both word and deed. The commanding, transforming reality is a shaping power; it shapes one's beliefs about that reality and when it works through persons it shapes the community of justice and love.

There is no such thing as poetry without poems, art without paintings, architecture without buildings, and there is no such thing as an enduring faith without beliefs. The *living* spirit, says the poet Schiller, creates and molds.

There can be no reliable faith for the free unless there are faith-ful men and women who form the faith into beliefs, who test and criticize the beliefs, and who then transform and transmit the beliefs. This process of forming and transforming the beliefs of the free faith is a process of discussion; it is a cooperative endeavor in which people surrender to the commanding, transforming reality. The only way men and women can reliably form and transform beliefs is through the sharing of tradition and new insights and through the cooperative criticism and testing of tradition and insight. In other words, people must sincerely work with each other in order to give reliable form and expression to faith. This is the only way freedom *from* tyranny can be fulfilled in freedom *with* justice and truth.

Belief in merely individualistic, fissiparous freedom of faith can lead only to vapidity, to a faith in "I know not what," to faith in the arbitrary.

Faith in the knowledge about the commanding, sustaining, transforming reality cannot be "just any faith." If it is to make a difference, if it is to enable us to distinguish between ourselves and Nazis, then it must have a definite, particular form. Religious liberals who say that religious liberalism encourages people merely to think as they please no longer believe there is a commanding reality. They have become "faith-fully" neutral, and this neutrality is only a halfway station (if not already a camouflage) for an unexamined faith, for an unreliable, destructive faith. Neither the vague nor the neutral "faith" can be overcome except in a faith-ful community.

The free church is that community which is committed to determining what is rightly of ultimate concern to persons of free faith. It is a community of the faithful and a community of sinners. When alive, it is the community in which men and women are called to seek fulfillment by the surrender of their lives to the control of the commanding, sustaining, transforming reality. It is the community in which women and men are called to recognize and abandon their ever-recurrent reliance upon the unreliable. It is the community in which the life-spirit of faith tries to create and mold life-giving, life-transforming beliefs, the community in which persons open themselves to God and each other and to commanding, sustaining, transforming experiences from the past, appropriating, criticizing, and transforming tradition and giving that tradition as well as newborn faith the occasion to become relevant to the needs of a time. These roots of faith grow in the individual as one participates in the worshiping, educating, socially active fellowship of the church. And certainly if they do not grow in the individual they will not grow in the family, if they do not grow in the family they will not grow in the community, and if they do not grow in the community they will not grow in the nation and the world.

Now the idea of forming a community of such a faith is a bold venture. It means that women and men must be willing not only to recognize their frustration of the transforming reality, but also to re-form themselves and their faith. As we have suggested, not every kind of freedom is permissible in this kind of community. Doctrinal tests are not the way to determine the character of the community, but if the community possesses no recognizable form and criterion (except that it offers absolute freedom), then it will be utterly undependable. It will degenerate into faith-ful and ethical neutrality.

An example of this degeneration recently came to light in a prominent congregation. The minister had been preaching vigorously and calling for action against race discrimination. Certain members of the board of trustees in the church did not like this sort of interpretation of our common humanity; apparently they thought that freedom of faith should permit freedom to believe in race discrimination. They called their minister to task and charged him with jeopardizing the principles of a free church. He was wrong, they said, in saying that the church must stand unambiguously against race discrimination. Some people in the group made this assumption, they admitted, but some did not. Therefore, if the church was to remain a free fellowship, these different ideas about race discrimination should be given equal respect. Otherwise, freedom of faith would be violated! In effect these "Christians" wanted their church to go the straight and narrow path—between right and wrong. They repudiated the "faith for the free" by trying to conceal injustice behind a simulated ethical neutrality.

A faith that creates no community of faith and a faith that assumes no definite form is not only a protection against any explicit faith, it is probably also a protection for a hidden idolatry of blood or state or economic interest, a protection for some kind of tyranny. It is not the faith of the free. The faith of free persons must tangibly make them free in a community of human dignity and equal justice.

The community of justice and love is not an ethereal fellowship that is *above* the conflicts and turmoils of the world. It is one that takes shape in nature and history, one that requires the achievement of freedom with respect to material resources as well as with respect to spiritual resources. Indeed, the one kind of freedom is not genuine without the other. Freedom requires a body as well as a spirit. We live not by spirit alone. A purely spiritual religion is a purely spurious religion; it is one that exempts its believer from surrender to the sustaining, transforming reality that demands the community of justice and love. This sham spirituality, far more than materialism, is the great enemy of religion.

Now, anything that exists effectively in history must have form and the creation of form requires power, not only the power of thought (mentioned above) but also the power of organization and the organization of power. There is no such thing as goodness as such; there is no such thing as a good man or woman as such. There is only the good spouse, the good worker, the good employer, the good churchperson, the good citizen. The decisive forms of goodness in society are institutional forms. No one can properly put faith in merely individual virtue, even though that is a prerequisite for societal virtues. The faith of the free must express itself in societal forms, in the forms of education, in economic and societal organization, in political organization. Without these, freedom and justice in community are impossible.

The faith of a church or of a nation is an adequate faith only when it inspires persons to give of their time and energy to shape the various institutions—social, economic, and political—of the common life. A faith in the commanding, sustaining, transforming reality is one that shapes history. Any other faith is thoroughly undependable; it is also impotent. It is not a faith that molds history. It is the "faith" that enables history to crush humanity.

Here we confront a fact that can be ignored only at our peril. The creation of justice in community requires the organization of power. Through the organization of power the free person ties into history; otherwise one can not achieve freedom *in history*. Injustice in community is a form of power, an abuse of power, and justice is an exercise of just and lawful institutional power.

The kind of freedom that expresses itself only within the family and within the narrow confines of one's daily work is not the faith of the free. It is as lopsided as the other kind of "freedom" that tries to express itself only in larger public affairs and forgets that the health of the body politic depends on the health and faith of its individual members. At best it creates and expresses cloistered virtues of loyalty, honesty, and diligence. This kind of faith can be oblivious of the injustices of the economic and political order; it can be a form of assistance to the powers of evil in public life and consequently also in the private life.

Today we are living in a time of sifting. No mere "return to religion" in the conventional sense will give us the vision or the power to match the demands. "Return to religion" as usually understood restores only the ashes and not the fires of faith. In a time when we must determine whether we will have "One World or None," only a costing commitment to a tough faith in a commanding, sustaining, transforming power of God will even start us on the steep path toward a world in which there will be room for people of free faith. If we can get such a world without a struggle for justice, it will, like an unexamined faith, not be worth having. In fact, we shall not have it for long—for the Lord of history will not fail nor faint till he has set justice in the earth, until he has burst the cruel yoke asunder and given liberty to the captive and to them that are oppressed. This is the Lord of whom it is commanded, Thou shalt love the Lord thy God with all thy heart, and with all thy soul, and with all thy mind, and with all thy strength. Would any other Lord, of any name or no name, be lovable? If the men and women of a free faith do not love *that* commanding, sustaining, transforming reality, what else in heaven or earth could they or should they love? What else could they have faith in?

Neither Mere Morality
Nor Mere God

This short essay, originally published in 1959, affirms that theology and ethics must go hand in hand. While conservatives have often treated religious beliefs as if they were disconnected from social and cultural beliefs, liberals have often reduced religious beliefs to ethics. Both are mistaken, for one fails to reckon with our need for relevance and the other with our need for transcendence. Adams commented on Matthew Arnold's definition of religion as "morality touched by emotion" and concluded with his own statement of liberal Christian faith.—GKB

The late Dean William W. Fenn of Harvard Divinity School used to tell of a snatch of heated conversation between two students he once overheard as he passed through the corridor of Andover Hall at the Divinity School. Attempting to bring an argument to a triumphant conclusion, the one student said, "All you have is *mere* morality." To this the other student replied scornfully, "And all you have is *mere* God."

These two epithets, "mere morality" and "mere God,"

adumbrate two aspects of the religious mentality which, as each of the students from his perspective implied, should never be allowed to stand in simple opposition or separation. These epithets are of course little more than polemical weapons; but they do point to a fundamental and perennial question, that of the relation between fact and value. Are the high values that elicit human commitment merely human, or are they more than human in their rootage and sanction?

The British philosopher F. H. Bradley once commented on Matthew Arnold's claim that "religion is morality touched with emotion." In fairness to Arnold it should be recalled that he went beyond this definition in his description of God as "the power not ourselves working for righteousness." But here is Bradley's comment on the definition of religion just cited:

> "Is there a God?" asks the reader. "O, yes," replies Mr. Arnold, "and I can verify him in experience." "And what is he then?" cries the reader. "Be virtuous and as a rule you will be happy," is the answer. "Well, and God?" "That is God," says Mr. Arnold, "there is no deception and what more do you want?"

Then Bradley goes on to say:

> I suppose we do want a good deal more. Most of us, certainly the public which Mr. Arnold ad-

dressed, want something they can worship; and they will not find that in a hypostatized copy-book heading, which is not much more adorable than "Honesty is the best policy," or "Handsome is that handsome does," or various other edifying maxims which have not yet come to an apotheosis.

Religious commitment issues from the declarative into the imperative mood, from recognition of divine Fact that defines and redefines and sustains virtue. This is the sense of Baron Friedrich von Hügel's assertion that "religion has primarily to do with is-ness and only secondarily to do with ought-ness."

This pointing beyond "ought-ness" to "is-ness" is characteristic not only of religion. Science is also concerned in the first instance with fact. Scientists as such are not primarily interested in the social change for good which their scientific discoveries will make possible. That interest belongs to the applied sciences. Scientists are primarily concerned to know the truth about the world as they find it, and they are not as scientists primarily concerned with what they ought to do with or about it. Religion and science in their differing ways seek reliable fact.

Accordingly, religious faith is a response to that which is held to be ultimately reliable. Christian faith finds the ultimately reliable fact in the meaning-giving, sustaining, fellowship-creating, transforming power to which Jesus of Nazareth responded and which is available ("near at hand") in the Reign of God. This "object" of faith is neither "mere morality" nor "mere God" if they are viewed as opposite or separate. It is just because of this that Dean Fenn was fond of telling his story.

Christianity is not "morality touched with emotion." Nor is it, strictly speaking, a mystical religion. It is a prophetic, that is, a historical religion; it summons men and women to an encounter with, a response to, a living God, the Lord of History, who has "spoken and speaks" to and in history; it points to an initiative that is not of human making and to a response that is concrete and incarnational in the perennial struggle against the forces of evil in humanity and in history. Its mode is existential more than it is discursively argumentative. We should dwell for a moment here on the prophetic sense of urgency with respect to this demand for the concrete.

In a recent poll at Harvard College a substantial proportion of undergraduates, according to the *Harvard Crimson*, "presented a God whose substance is so tenuous and vague that, like certain very rare gases, it becomes highly enigmatic to say that He is 'there' at all. Such a being certainly seems incapable of having much more of an effect on human life than the normal inhalation of argon." This kind of God is no longer a concrete presence. It is the dead end of the alley of pale abstraction. Actually, however, the abstractionist conception of God can point to a noble, if erstwhile forgotten, heritage. Rational clarity and consistency again and again, in the very name of a God of order, must enter the scene in order to correct the arbitrariness, the naive anthropomorphism, the superstitions, of "faith." On the other hand, this rational thrust can create a vacuum that the writer in *The Crimson* describes. Arguments about the existence of God can end up here. But the vacuum of abstractionism generally does not last. It gets filled up with half-gods. Some concrete, some commanding power such as the nation, the white pigment, or the flesh-pots of suburbia, will project and occupy a throne. A new superstition becomes the subject of faith. Thus humans show themselves to be incurably, and even self-destructively, "religious."

One can observe in the history of the ancient Hebrew religion this oscillation between devotion to a distant, if universal, God and the demand for something more immediate and concrete. The German philosopher Schelling, recognizing this oscillation in the history of religions, called for a transcending of the *universality* of abstract monotheism and the idolatrous *concreteness* of polytheism. He found this in the New Testament. Martin Buber has frequently commented on the viability that the Christian conception of God enjoys by virtue of the centrality of Jesus in Christian devotion.

The liberal Christian outlook is directed to a Power that is living, that is active in a love seeking concrete manifestation, and that finds decisive response in the living posture and gesture of Jesus of Nazareth. In a world that has with some conscientiousness turned against this kind of witness and its vocabulary, the effect of this witness will in a special way depend on the quality of its costingness in concrete action and upon its relevance to the history that is in the making. To say this is only to say that the truly reliable God is the Lord of History and also that our sins will find us out. Yet, this Lord of History has given us a world in which the possibility of new beginnings is ever present along with the judgment that is always upon us. To this Lord of History Jesus responded with his message and demonstration of hope in concert with sacrifice.

The Changing Reputation
of Human Nature

*In his Berry Street Conference address, given at the May
Meetings of the American Unitarian Association in 1941,
Adams undertook a far-reaching critique of liberal religious
views of human nature. Because liberalism did not reckon
with the tragic dimension of history and did not face squarely
the reality of evil, it was caught in a "cultural lag"; in consequence it was ineffectual in the face of the political and cultural crises of the twentieth century. Adams sought to shift
liberal religious thought from rationalism—giving primacy
to the intellect—to voluntarism—giving primacy to the will.
We are "fated to be free," said Adams, yet we are subject to
the limitations of time and history. Thus decision and commitment become central issues of contemporary faith.
Adams's lecture is here abridged.—GKB*

Ancient Greek Views of Humanity

Nietzsche pointed out to us, some time ago, that in the
ancient Greek tradition we find two typical estimates of
human nature and the human situation. One view is
associated with the classical philosophers, and is usu-

ally called the intellectualistic or rationalistic view, the Apollonian view. According to this view, reason is the masterful principal of creation, and the cosmos is a moving shadow of a world of eternal ideas, essences, or forms. Correspondingly, our primary, distinguishing faculty is our reason, and through it we can release a vitality that will enable us to achieve control of ourselves and of the human situation by subjecting them to clearly envisaged forms. What is to be especially noted here is the tendency of this intellectualistic view, first, to interpret existence in terms of a rational, unified, harmonious structure, and, second, to exalt the cognitive, nonaffective aspects of the human psyche. The conjunction of these two elements leads to a preoccupation with the forms and structures of being and to a "theoretical attitude of distance" that aims at the development of the form and harmony of the Olympian calm. Thus the vitality of nature, humanity, and history is presumed, but creativity is identified with the operations of reason.

The other view of human nature in the Hellenic tradition to which Nietzsche drew our attention interprets existence more in terms of vitality than of form, a vitality that is both creative and destructive, that imbues every form but that also eludes and bursts the bounds of every structure. It is associated with one of the major traditions in popular Greek religion, with certain pre-Socratic philosophers very close to this religious tradition, and in certain respects, with the great tragedians. It has usually been characterized as the Dionysian view.

In recent decades this view and certain modern variations of it have been spoken of as "voluntarism."

In general, this view exalts the dynamic aspects of existence; therefore it conceives of humanity's proper goal as the fulfillment of the life-giving powers inherent in existence. But here the elements of struggle, contradiction, and tragedy, rather than the element of harmony, are emphasized. Thus in popular Greek thought and even among certain of the élite, a large place is assigned to Fate. We are believed to be confronted by divine and demonic forces that either support and inspire or thwart and pervert us in our attempt to fulfill our destiny. Although there is here a keen sense of tragedy, we do not in this view necessarily lose our dignity and worth. Quite the contrary. In the great Greek tragedies, for example, the tragic element is discovered at the very point at which human greatness and the divine sphere come into conflict. It is precisely human greatness that makes possible tragic guilt and self-destruction. Indeed, according to this view, not only are we plagued by a Fate that drives us to tragic guilt and self-destruction; but even the gods are subject to it, since no one of them can be identified with the highest principle. Fate is considered to be sovereign over both ourselves and the gods just because it is viewed as a causal manifestation of a primordial creative principle. The point to be stressed, however, is that humanity is here understood in terms of the dignity and fate of a human agent confronted by a will or power that cannot be created or controlled by any merely rational technique. The tragic process is master of all forms, causing them to undergo change and transformation and even destruction.

Judeo-Christian Views

It should be clear that we cannot properly understand the third influential attitude toward humanity and existence—the Judeo-Christian view—if we interpret it as constituting a complete contrast with the Greek views of life. It is true that there is little in common between the Jewish-and-early-Christian view and the Apollonian attitude. Insofar as Matthew Arnold confines his attention to these two points of view he is a reliable guide when he characterizes the differences between Hellenism and Hebraism. In addition to the differences Arnold describes, we should note that another difference between the Judeo-Christian and the sophisticated Greek outlook is to be discerned in their contrasting views of time and history; the one looked on history as "forward moving" toward a particular End (*eschaton*), while the other viewed it as cyclic.

On the other hand, the Greek Dionysian view and the Judeo-Christian attitude bear a resemblance to each other in their possession of a "tragic sense of life," as well as in their emphasis upon the dynamic elements in the world and in human life. According to the Judeo-Christian view, God is a righteous will fulfilling its purpose in history; humanity and nature are fallen; our natural will is at variance with the divine will; our sin, guilt, and conflict with the principalities and powers of this world are an inextricable part of human experience. Thus, in both the Greek tragic view and the Jewish prophetic and primitive Christian outlook, there is an awareness of an ontologically grounded tendency in humanity toward rebellion, perversion and self-destruction. Moreover, in both views the attention is centered upon the dynamic, creative-destructive aspects of humanity and upon the affective aspects of the psyche.

Yet, there are also certain fundamental differences to be observed between the Judeo-Christian and the Greek "tragic" view. Two of these differences may be noted here. The first has to do with the ultimate valuation they place on existence. The Judeo-Christian doctrine of creation involves the idea that in substance the world is good because it is God's creation. Nothing in existence is absolutely antidivine, for in order to exist an object must contain something of the divine. *Esse est bonum qua esse.* The Christian confession: "I believe in God the Father Almighty, the Creator of heaven and earth" has this idea as its real import. Even suffering may be a means of grace. Indeed, the Cross itself is the highest revelation of the character of God, for through it divine providence overcomes sin and death. Likewise, the Pauline belief in original sin is outweighed by the emphasis on providence and the hope of redemption. Thus God is beyond tragedy; and, ultimately, existence and history are not tragic. On the other hand, the Greek popular view, from pre-Homeric times onward, was unable to find a principle of transcendence beyond the tragedy of existence. This view finds philosophical expression in the famous fragment of Anaximander: "Things perish into those things from which they have their birth, as it is ordained; for they pay to one another the penalty of their injustice according to the order of time." For Anaximander, "the separate existence of things is, so to speak, a wrong, a transgression which they must expiate by their destruction."

The other major difference between the Judeo-Christian and the Dionysian view concerns their contrasting attitudes toward reason and morality. The Dionysian view was strongly characterized by "enthusiastic" irrationalism and amoralism, defects made familiar to most of us through the diatribes of Euripides against Dionysianism. The Judeo-Christian mentality in its formative period made no virtue of irrationalism, and it strongly opposed amoralism. Whether we think of the Old Testament prophets, the writers of the Wisdom literature, or of the great rabbis of normative Judaism, whether we think of Jesus, Paul, the author of the Fourth Gospel, or of the Greek fathers or Augustine—the main line of the Christian tradition—we find no exaltation of irrationalism, and we find a great emphasis placed on conformity to the righteous will of God. With respect to the attitude toward reason, it is no accident that the Christian outlook could be merged with Greek theology. It is largely because of this coming together of

Judeo-Christian voluntarism and Greek intellectualism that Christianity became the transmitter of much of the best in both the ancient Semitic and the ancient Greek traditions.

Much of the history of thought in the West may in its broader perspectives be interpreted as a history of the combination of, and the tension and interplay between, the three attitudes toward existence that we have briefly described. In view of the fact, however, that the *pagan* tragic view was effectually overcome in the Middle Ages, modern thought about humanity and existence for the most part represents an interplay between only two of these attitudes, the Greek intellectualist and the Judeo-Christian voluntarist view. The views that prevailed in the Middle Ages, in the Renaissance and the Reformation, and even in the periods of the Enlightenment and of Romanticism are to be interpreted as modern developments, combinations or perversions of motifs already present in these ancient Greek and Hebrew traditions. The increasingly dominant force in modern Western culture, however, has been the rationalistic tradition.

Modern Developments

The modern development of intellectualism must be understood as a reaction against the extreme forms of voluntarism. In large degree the Renaissance was a revolt against the obscurantism and authoritarianism the

Middle Ages and also against certain forms of earlier voluntarism (though it must be added that the Renaissance was also voluntaristic in some respects). Likewise, intellectualism in later centuries represents a revolt against the extreme forms of voluntarism found in orthodox Calvinism and Lutheranism.

Indeed, religious liberalism itself can be understood in its proper perspective only when interpreted as an aspect of this opposition. In religious liberalism the rationalistic view of human nature and of the human situation appeared as a revolt against the older forms of authoritarianism, a revolt in the name of the principles of freedom of mind and freedom of conscience. But concomitantly the liberal movement represented also a revolt against the Protestant dogma of the total depravity of human nature, that is, against a depraved, lopsided, rationalized form of the Christian doctrine of original sin. In short, it was a revolt against a voluntarism that had gone to seed.

The fruits of this struggle and of the great humanitarian impulse of the nineteenth century represent no mean cultural accomplishment. This fact can scarcely be overemphasized. Moreover, contemporary Protestantism owes to religious liberalism the social emphasis that in the past century has been reintroduced into Protestant thought and action.

But, unfortunately, not all the fruits issuing from the new movement were actually intended or expected by its proponents. Nor was the movement able to maintain in the main body of its adherents the prophetic power of its early days. The new intellectualism, which in its early stages was powerfully dynamic, more and more moved in the direction of emphasizing again the cognitive aspects of human nature—"the theoretical attitude of distance"—and thus neglected the affective side of human nature and "the attitude of decision." The influence of the scientific method, despite its value in other respects, played no small role in accelerating this tendency.

As a consequence, the emphasis on the quality of the will, on the disposition of the *entire* personality, was replaced by a onesided emphasis on "reason." The attitude of Greek rationalism, as mediated through Stoicism and scholasticism and transformed by modern rationalism, was taking the place of the older Augustinian emphasis on the will and the affections. Here we find, then, the element that has given liberal religion its reputation for being intellectual. The appeal to affective experience, the belief in the necessity for conversion, and the use of the emotive symbols of the religious tradition were more and more deprecated. Thus religious liberalism, in the name of *intellectual* integrity, tended to neglect the deeper levels both of the human consciousness and of reality itself. As a consequence, it gradually became associated with an ascetic attitude toward the imagination as well as toward enthusiasm and gripping loyalities. Instead of confronting people with the demand of inner commitment of the ideals of prophetic religion, it more and more provided a cosmic or religious sanction for the interests of a "respectable" group. Conversion was relegated to the underprivileged classes or taken as a sign of ignorance. In the end "the attitude of distance" won the day, and liberalism achieved poise by living at the low temperature of "detached, middle-class common sense," as Whitehead called it.

These tendencies were not the consequence of a loss of faith. They were merely the negative aspects of a new faith. Nor was this a faith merely in human reason or in humanity alone. It was a faith that found its support in a new idea of the character of the universe and of humanity as a part of that universe.

This faith and its supporting conception of the universe is what is generally referred to when the modern historian of culture speaks of liberalism. It is against this type of liberalism and its contemporary residues that much of the current criticism of religious liberalism is directed. Insofar as it is valid, this criticism does not involve a repudiation of the liberal idea of liberating the human spirit from the bondage of economic, social, and ecclesiastical tyrannies. Instead, it is directed against the view of human nature and of the nature of reality that is explicit in eighteenth- and nineteenth-century liberalism and which is still implicit in much liberal thought of today. Hence, it is directed also against the tendency of this type of liberalism to become associated too closely with the interests of one class in society.

Pre-established Harmony

Dean William W. Fenn once pointed out that the favorite concept of modern rationalistic liberalism is its belief in the unified structure of the world. This belief is the modern counterpart of the Greek rationalistic view of ultimate reality as a unified pattern behind phenomena, a pattern that is viewed as the source of vitality and with which the rational soul feels itself akin. It has found a great variety of expression, as in Descartes's faith in the existence of a divine power that harmonizes both mind and nature, or in Spinoza's view that thought and extension are different attributes of the same substance and that God is the substance, or in Leibniz's theory of a pre-established harmony that preserves unity despite apparent diversity, or in his view that the individual is a unified whole within the macrocosm. Jung's psychology is one of the more influential current forms of this basic view.

We are all familiar with the result of this tendency. Because of the pre-established harmony, separative individualism was given a divine sanction, and the modern liberal's overoptimism about human nature, its possibilities for growth, and its progressive and ultimate perfectibility was born. Mandeville does, to be sure, recognize the contrast between the selfish desire of the bourgeois person and the desire for order and education. But he resolves the conflict by appealing to the pre-established harmony: hence, he says, private vices are public virtues. Shaftesbury and Hutcheson discover a moral sense in everybody. This moral sense, they say, is an invariant norm, the violation of which would alone introduce discord. Helvetius even goes so far as to assert that self-love leads ultimately to the love of others. Condillac says that the brain is a *tabula rasa*, but the laws of matter operative in brain vibrations will bring forth truth. How? Through the pre-established harmony. And many of the scientists of the eighteenth and nineteenth centuries, following the lead of Francis Bacon, believed that if only the scientists would individually specialize and then pool their findings the reign of humankind would be ushered in. Finally, liberal economics proclaimed the faith that if markets were made free and state interference were reduced to a minimum, the rationality of economic forces would do the rest and harmonious well-being for everybody would ensue. This view was supported by the doctrine of the harmony of interests, according to which the individual could be relied on, without external control, to promote the interests of the community for the reason that those interests were thought to be identical with the individual's own. The harmony was believed to be none the less real if those concerned were unconscious of it. The pre-established harmony would operate willy-nilly. According to Adam Smith, the popularizer of the doctrine of the harmony of interests, the individual "neither intends to promote the public interest, nor knows how much he is promoting it. . . . He intends only his own gain, and he is in this, as in many other cases, led by an invisible hand to promote an end which was no part of his intention."

Out of roots such as these grew the ideas of growth, progress, and perfectibility characteristic of the secular as well as of the religious liberalism of the eighteenth and nineteenth centuries. In some quarters, these ideas were related to a new faith in humanity; in others they were related to a thoroughly worked-out philosophy of history; and in still others they were rooted in a belief in "cosmic progress." Within these variations, there were still others. Some liberals, for example, emphasized the natural power of reason, while others, under the influence of romanticism, emphasized the natural power of sympathy. In 1885 belief in "the progress of mankind onward and upward forever" became one of the main articles of the Unitarian faith. And, as an eminent Unitarian historian says, Dr. James Freeman Clark "leaves us in no doubt concerning the importance" he ascribed to the famous Point Five: "He did not intend 'the Progress of Mankind' to be an *omnium gatherum*, or an anti-climax; on the contrary, he regarded the belief in human progress as an essential and a summary of a true Liberal's religion." Dr. Clark's sermon in which the "Five Points of the New Theology" were first set forth concludes with this affirmation: "The one fact which is written on nature and human life, which accords with all we see and know, is the fact of progress; and this must be accepted as *the purpose* of the creation."

Historical Consciousness

But as the great liberal historian Ernest Troeltsch said, history is something "given," and the forces that operate there share the alogical character inherent in existence itself. This alogical character of history is manifest both in necessity and in freedom. Neither the necessity nor the freedom can be understood merely in terms of reason and its self-evident premises. In the first place, knowledge of the character of that necessity can be acquired only by observing it inductively and not by deduction from *a priori* principles. In the second place, the very fact of human freedom gives to history a singularity peculiar to all human creations. "In history," as Troeltsch says, "a qualitative unity and originality is assumed to be originally given . . . which may be called fate, destiny, creation, or something else." He speaks of this aspect of history as metalogical and not logical. For whereas organic nature is practically enclosed within the biological circle of birth, growth, procreation, and death, history does not repeat itself—it generates novelty. And because of this also, it cannot be interpreted in strictly rationalistic terms. As Bergson and Whitehead (as well as Troeltsch) have pointed out, strict rationalism precludes the possibility of novelty.

Now, there are certain implications for the nature of humanity that must be seen to follow from the fact that history is the realm of both necessity and freedom. Humanity is fated as well as free. As Wilhelm von Humboldt puts it, "humanity always ties on to what lies at hand."

Certain fateful conditioning factors always operate in the individual as well as in society. Humanity must act in terms of the historical process and of the psychophysical organism. Our actions must be of a certain kind in order to be relevant and also in order that we may avoid destruction. We cannot act merely in accordance with logical canons of an *a priori* order. Even our ethical ideals emerge through our experience of being and of history. In this sense, it may be said that "being is older than value." Yet, despite these conditioning factors, humanity is fated also to be free; we are compelled to make decisions. For we can transcend our situation and in some measure we can freely change it; we can even change ourselves. As creative beings we can act to preserve or increase, destroy or pervert, mutuality—though it must be remembered also that conditions over which we have little control may affect the results of our action. We are fatefully caught in history, both as individuals and as members of a group, and we are also able to be creative in history.

Through the use of this creative freedom, humanity expresses the highest form of vitality that existence permits. Indeed, since this creativity is a manifestation of a divinely given and divinely renewing power, we say that humanity is created in the image of God, that is, we participate in the divine creativity. This and not reason alone is the basis for the liberal's faith in humanity, and no change in the reputation of human nature could involve a denial of this fact without also repudiating the very essence of the liberal understanding of humanity.

Because of this freedom, human history not only exhibits a singularity that transcends all *a priori* conceptions of the intellect; it also provides a more complex and spiritual form of conflict than to be found on the level of nature. For history is a theater of conflict in which the tensions between the will to mutuality and the will to power appear in their most subtle and perverse forms. In short, history is tragic. Let it be said immediately that this does not mean merely that people violate the moral code or disobey the law. That they do these things is obvious and universally recognized. The changing reputation of human nature does not depend upon any such "discovery."

Progress and Tragedy in History

It is at this point that we come to the consideration of the major deficiencies in the older liberal doctrines of human nature and progress. These deficiencies can be brought into bold relief by showing concretely what is meant by the assertion that history is tragic. We shall use the liberal epoch as an illustration of this view of history, not because that epoch is different from other epochs as a revelation of the nature of history, but rather because the tragic outcome of liberalism in the present crisis presents the major problem confronting contemporary society and also because liberalism provides certain of the principles that are of decisive positive significance for the continued development of a democratic society and of liberal religion. In dealing with these problems we shall have to go over some very familiar ground. But it would seem worthwhile to do this, not only in order to show how the monistic, liberal doctrines of humanity and progress actually contributed to the tragic outcome of the liberal epoch but also in the order later to indicate how a voluntaristic interpretation of human nature and history purports to correct the deficiencies of the "harmonistic" conception.

When we say that history is tragic, we mean that the perversions and failures in history are associated precisely with the highest creative powers of humanity and thus with our greatest achievements. One might call this the Oedipus motif in the sphere of history: nemesis is very often encountered almost simultaneously with the seemingly highest achievement. The very means and evidences of progress turn out again and again to be also the instruments of perversion or destruction. The national culture, for example, is the soil from which issue cherished treasures of a people, their language, their poetry, their music, their common social heritage. Yet nationalism is also one of the most destructive forces in the whole of human history. Progress in transportation has assisted tremendously in the raising of the standard of living: yet it has produced also a mobility in our cultural life which has brought in its train a new rootlessness and instability. Improved means of printing have made the treasures of the printed page available even to those who run as they read. But it has also made possible the appearance of the irresponsible manipulators of the idea industries, with the consequence that literacy is now also a powerful instrument for demagogy and the corruption of taste. The growth of a machine civilization has made available to the peasant objects that sovereigns used to pine for; yet "the machine doth man unking," and it has necessitated so rapid an urbanization of the population that a sense of community has been destroyed for millions of people, and intimate, colorful family life has become largely a rural phenomenon.

Or, consider another aspect of progress. There is no such thing as a unilinear development in the area of moral achievement. We see this in the fact that each generation has to acquire wisdom over again, and within this process "the war of the generations" arises. The child of the Philistine becomes a Bohemian, and his child becomes a communist. The mystical Body of Christ becomes an autocratic ecclesiastical hierarchy, and this in turn gives place to a spiritual anarchy or a militant secularism. There is progress here, regress and a new attempt or perversion there; one year a Revolution for "the Rights of Man," but four years later a Reign of Terror and then a Napoleonic era; an American Revolution then, Daughters of the American Revolution now. Certainly, if there is progress, it is no simple configuration of upward trends. At times, it looks more like a thing of shreds and patches. The general tendency of liberalism has been to neglect this tragic factor of history. It is true that most of the theorists of liberalism were definitely pessimistic concerning humanity's worthiness of being entrusted with concentrated political power, but the general and prevailing trend of their thinking was nevertheless lop-sidedly optimistic.

It is true also that in the heyday of the idea of progress a few expressed skepticism concerning the progress "assured by the trend of natural forces," but they were given little heed. A poet here and there, an orthodox Calvinist or a cranky social prophet spoke out, but the idea that some people when released from bondage to superstition or to political and ecclesiastical domination, might use their newly acquired freedom and reason to build a new Bastille does not seem to have occurred to many.

Now, what should be noticed here is that this contradiction in human nature derives from the fact that human will is a decisive element in human structure. And it is a will that is ambiguous in character. We can use our freedom by expressing a will to mutuality, but we can also abuse it by exercising a will to power. Freedom and liberation is therefore both the basis of meaning and the occasion for the destruction of meaning. Here we see again the tragic nature of the human condition. The tragedy does not derive merely from the fact that humanity carries an inheritance from the jungle within. It derives also (and primarily) from the fact that we have a freedom that we did not have in the jungle, a freedom to exercise the infinitely higher powers of human nature in terms of creative love, and a freedom to waste them in mere lassitude and triviality, or to pervert them for the sake of a will to power.

It is this coexistence in humanity of the possibility of using our freedom *ad majorem gloriam dei* and the possibility of perverting it to our own destructive ends that constitutes the deepest contradiction of our nature. And this contradiction is no merely human, subjective phenomenon. As Martin Luther suggests, humanity is the *Schauplatz* of opposing cosmic forces, the forces of love and of power. The contradiction penetrates our innermost spiritual life. It goes to the very center of our being; and it reaches out through the individual and permeates all our social relations. It is not, as the Marxists contend, merely a precipitant of the structure of society.

The Contradictions in Human Nature

It was in connection with the sort of interpretation here set forth that the historic Judeo-Christian doctrine of sin was developed. The "orthodox" theory of "original sin," because of its association with the notion of Adam's Fall "in whom we sinned all" as well as with an ascetic conception of sex, has been rightly abandoned by religious liberals. It is doubtful, however, if there is any word available that has more profound metaphysical implications than the word "sin," for the word has the theonomous reference necessary for any truly theological category. But, whether liberals use the word "sin" or not, they cannot correct this "too jocund" view of life until they recognize that there is in human nature a deep-seated and universal tendency for both individuals and groups to ignore the demands of mutuality and thus to waste freedom or abuse it by devotion to the idols of the tribe, the theater, the cave, and the market-place. The old triumvirate of tyrants in the human soul, the *libido sciendi*, the *libido sentiendi*, and the *libido dominandi*, is just as powerful today as it ever was, and no one can ignore its tyranny with impunity. It cannot be denied that religious liberalism has neglected these aspects of human nature in its zeal to proclaim the spark of divinity in humanity. We may call these tendencies by any name we wish, but we do not escape their destructive influence by a conspiracy of silence concerning them. Certainly, the practice of shunning the word "sin" because "it makes one feel gloomy and pious," has little more justification than the use of the ostrich method in other areas of life.

Obviously, a correction here does not involve any lending of support to the old view of "total depravity," at least not among liberals. We ought to have enough faith in humanity and God to believe that even a "realistic and credible doctrine of humanity" will not separate us from the love of God. Certainly, we ought to be willing to take the risk that we would incur by giving more serious consideration than we have in recent years to the sinful side of human nature, and even to the biblical myth of the Fall as a description of the contradictions in human nature.

But extreme pessimism is not the only danger of the tragic view of life that is now emerging. Just as rationalism had its characteristic besetting sin, namely, "feeling terribly at ease in Zion" and "cuddling up to the Almighty," so voluntarism has its own peculiar danger. Certain types of voluntarism, it must be remembered, have often been infected with irrationalism. Indeed, they have even exalted irrationalism into a virtue. Duns Scotus illustrates this tendency when he urged acceptance of the Catholic faith without question and without reference to reason. National Socialism took the same attitude of authoritarian subjection to blood and soil. Observers from the Orient have long noted this tendency to irrationalism in the Christian Occident. Charles Chauncy valiantly opposed it in the New Lights, and many oppose it today as it appears in new nationalisms and new spiritual fanaticisms of various stripes. But such irrationalism is not the only alternative to rationalism. We find keen rational analysis in great historic exemplars of voluntarism—for example, most of all in the Buddha, and to a marked degree in St. Paul and St. Augustine, or—to cite three modern examples—in Jonathan Edwards, Ernst Troeltsch, and Rudolph Otto. What is needed, of course, is that combination of *logos* and *dynamis* that can effect a vitalizing tension between the attitude of distance and the attitude of decision.

One of the best characterizations of this sort of relation between the reason and the will is suggested in the metaphor repeated by most of the voluntarists of the Middle Ages and especially by the anti-Thomists; they compared reason to a torch lighting the paths ahead; and the will under God's grace, the whole self, they said, both guides the reason and chooses the path to be taken. We see, then, that a recognition of the large role of the will, a recognition of the fundamental significance of the basic orientation and predisposition of humanity, does not necessarily involve a deprecation of reason. Indeed, the voluntaristic theory of human nature is itself the result of an intellectual and rational analysis of the human condition.

The older liberalism underestimated the destructive possibilities of the contradictions in human nature and was thus unrealistic. It offered salvation through the "restraints of reason." But the "restraints of reason" are inadequate for entering the "war within the cave." Merely intellectual education is not enough. The world has many educated people who know how to reason, and they reason very well; but, curiously enough, many of them fail to examine the pre-established premises from which they reason, premises that turn out on examination to be antisocial, protective camouflages of power. Where our treasure is, there will our heart be also. And where our heart is, there will be our reason and our premises. The "theoretical attitude of distance" needs for its completion the existential "attitude of decision." St. Paul underlines this fact when he speaks of the foolishness of the wise. The element of conflict inherent in us and in human relations with our neighbors can, as St. Paul knew, be dealt with only by a regenerated will, a will committed to the principles of liberty and justice and love, a will prepared by a faith, a decision, a commitment sufficient to cope with the principalities and powers of the world.

Kant, who in this respect stands in the Pauline tradition, suggests that the *root* of evil must be touched. What is needed, he says, is not piecemeal reformation with minor adjustments of character and conduct, but an alteration of the basis of character and of the habitual way in which the mind works. Nor is this reformation a "conversion" of the evangelistic order, a conversion that takes place at one moment and is then complete: Martin Luther came much nearer to describing it when he said that our whole life should be a repentance (*metanoia*) that brings forth fruits meet for repentance. Nor is this conversion merely what we do with our solitariness. It is a conversion that affects our social relations and brings about some conversion in society.

Reason and Commitment

These principles can be stated in nontheological terms also. The way in which the reason operates depends upon the aims and interests around which the personality is organized. Morality has as its basis an underived commitment to certain guiding principles and purposes. Thus the basis of choice is not irrational in that the direction taken by choice is determined by the evidence or principles that can be applied. Accordingly, the decisive quality of a personality is its commitment, for the basic commitment determines the self and its interests, instead of being determined by them.

The way in which a personality will interpret its freedom and use its reason depends, then, upon the character of the self and upon its relation to and attitude toward the rest of reality. A readiness even to enter into discussion for the sake of reaching agreement (or of reaching at least a common understanding) depends upon our total character and not upon our intellectual capacities alone. It depends, in short, upon a proper relation to the creative ground of meaning and existence. Moreover, science as well as religion, politics as well as art, properly flourish only when the primary quality of human character or integrity is the foundation and when that integrity has a positive and critical relation to larger integrities, both social and metaphysical.

We have now seen the ways in which the rationalistic tradition has optimistically taken for granted the idea of unity in the world, in society, and in the structure of the individual psyche. We have also seen how it stresses the role of reason in such a way as to offer a truncated view of the functions operative in both society and the individual and also in such a way as to encourage both separative individualism and "the attitude of distance."

The voluntaristic outlook, we have seen, aims to correct and supplement this view by stressing the significance of the alogical factors in existence, in human nature and history, by emphasizing also "the tragic sense of life" arising from human entanglement within its deep-going conflicts, and by stressing the significance of the creative depths of the entire personality (and of the group to which it belongs) for the dynamic achievement of relevant and vigorous action.

Theology is, in the language of Bonaventura, "an affective science," the science of the love of God, and the function of the church is to bring people into communion with a group wherein the divine power of transformation and the ethical standards rooted in it are operative. When we say operative, we mean that this power is capable of changing people, of eliciting commitment to a way of life that makes a difference in their attitude toward themselves, others, and God; in short, it aids them in the achieving of voluntary community. Only by some such commitment can we, in Channing's words, be always young for liberty. And without such a commitment, we become content with "philosophic" objectivity and "distance" that insulate us from the source of true vitality, from openness to the power of the Spirit. We become attached to the forms that have given us our cherished securities; or, as Augustine puts it, we give our devotion to creatures rather than to the creative power from which issue all forms and all true vitality. We substitute our aspirations and "virtues," our reason and our moralism, for God's power and goodness. Thus our rationalism and our moralism "miss and distort reality and the real possibilities for improvement of the human situation." They give us a "poise" that freezes the knees and keeps us erect and "harmonious" in face of the divine demand for repentance, for change of heart and mind. The early Christians and the Protestant Reformers saw that the creative and redemptive power is not subject to domestication by means of these techniques. It breaks into a human situation destroying, transforming old forms and creating new ones, manifesting the expulsive and creative power of a new affection—the *amor dei*.

It is not reason alone, but reason inspired by "raised affections" that is necessary for salvation. We become what we love. Not that information and technique are dispensable. Even a St. Francis with commitment to the highest would be impotent when confronted with a case of appendicitis if he did not recognize the malady and did not know what to do. One sector of the problems of society is its intellectual problems—problems of statecraft, economics, pedagogy, and the like. Here no amount of good will alone can suffice. But something of the spirit of St. Francis is indispensable if the benefits of science and of society are to be in widest commonalty spread, and, for that matter, if even the intellectual problems are to be dealt with adequately. The desire to diagnose injustice as an intellectual problem as well as the power of action to achieve a new form of justice requires "raised affections," a vitality that can break through old forms of behavior and create new patterns of community. But the raising of the affections is a much harder thing to accomplish than even the education of the mind; it is especially difficult among those who think they have found security.

This element of commitment, of change of heart, of decision, so much emphasized in the Gospels, has been neglected by religious liberalism, and that is the prime source of its enfeeblement. We liberals are largely an uncommitted and therefore a self-frustrating people. Our first task, then, is to restore to liberalism its own dynamic and its own prophetic genius. We need conversion within ourselves. Only by some such revolution can we be seized by a prophetic power that will enable us to proclaim both the judgment and the love of God. Only by some such conversion can we be possessed by a love that will not let us go. And when that has taken place, we shall know that it is not our wills alone that have acted; we shall know that the ever-living Creator and Re-creator has again been brooding over the face of the deep and out of the depths bringing forth new life.

Music As a Means of Grace

Various forms of cultural expression are prominent in Adams's thought—literature, the visual arts, dance—but none is more prominent than music. He associated music with grace, the sense of a divine gift that enables good things to happen to us, and through us, to be communicated to others. In music grace becomes much more than an abstract idea; through its infinite and personally expressive varieties, music gives lively embodiment to grace. Adams called himself "a theologian of grace." We humans participate in the creation of meaning—for instance, by making music—but meaning is not finally a product of our devising but a divine gift, a transcendent reality in which we may participate. This essay was originally published in 1967.—GKB

When the morning stars sang together, and all the children of God shouted for joy.

—Job 38:7

And round the throne are four living creatures, and these four living creatures, each of them with six wings, day and night never cease to sing, "Holy,

Holy, Holy."

—Revelation 4:6-8

It is striking that the authors of these two passages cannot conceive of the beginning or the end of the world without music—at the beginning the morning stars sing together, and at the end the living creatures never cease to sing, "Holy, holy, holy." Music in all ages and cultures has been closely associated with religion, with primitive religion and with the higher religions. But it has a special connection with high religion.

No theologian in the history of Christianity has given a higher place to music than did Martin Luther. "I most heartily desire," he said, "that music, that divine and most precious gift, be praised and extolled before all people. I am so completely overwhelmed by the quantity and greatness of its excellence and virtues that I can find neither beginning nor end nor adequate words or expressions to say what I ought." "A person who does not regard music as a marvelous creation of God, must be a clodhopper indeed and does not deserve to be called a human being; [such a person] should be permitted to hear nothing but the braying of asses and the grunting of hogs." "Next to the Word of God," he said, "the noble art of music is the greatest treasure in the world. . . . There is no art its equal."

In Luther's view, the corrupting influence of Satan is helpless against this power, for "music alone can do what otherwise only theology can accomplish, namely quiet and cheer up the soul of man." Indeed, he says that music cannot be explained as an achievement of humanity but only as a gift, a creation of God given to humankind.

Luther even ventured to set forth a theology of music. Moreover, he helped to maintain the study of music as an integral part of education. "Those who have mastered this art are made of good stuff; they are fit for any task. . . . A teacher must be able to sing; otherwise I will not so much as look at him." Luther was the author of thirty-seven chorales. We do not know how many or for which of them he also wrote the music. But one could say that Luther sang the people into the Reformation. Certainly, Germany's accomplishments in music cannot be understood apart from him. Partly under his influence the organ became closely associated with the chorale, *Der Tanz im Himmel*.

Music has been associated not only with religion, but also with work, with play, with love both erotic and spiritual, with war, with Bacchanalian revelry, with wine, women, and song, and with all celebration whether solemn, festal, or inebriated. There are no strangers to music. Moreover, the question can be raised as to whether there is anything intrinsic in music that makes it religious or secular. What any people consider to be religious music is largely a matter of custom. The late Dr. Archibald Davison of the Harvard faculty used to remind us in the Harvard Glee Club that Handel's *Largo*, one of the most widely accepted pieces of so-called religious music, was originally incidental music for a scene in the opera *Xerxes*, a scene in which a man who has just eaten a heavy dinner sleeps it off sitting under a tree out in the garden. What is called religious music, or any other kind of music, is a matter of cultural conditioning. That proposition, I suppose, has become almost axiomatic for the musicologist.

Must we be content then to let the matter rest there? Plato, for one, would not accept such a view. Although he would by law exclude certain types of melody from the well-regulated state, he held that in authentic music there is an order that comports with ultimate reality, that consorts with the metrical harmony of the cosmos, and also with the order of the good. "The gods," he says, "who have been appointed to be our companions in the dance, have given us the pleasurable sense of harmony and rhythm; and so they stir us to life, and we follow them, joining together in dances and songs."

For Plato, authentic music also possesses a dimension of freedom. Through it people are freed from bondage to the pressing environment with its immediate claims. By means of music an ordered world, a higher and divine reality, is posited as a standard-giving environment. Whatever one may think of Plato's philosophy or metaphysics of music, he does suggest that something intrinsic, something more than merely culture-bound association, is to be encountered in music.

What a mysterious, almost fantastic, action is the creating and appreciation of music. In its purest form music is not a representational but rather a nonobjective, nonverbal world. It is a world of its own, almost a *creatio ex nihilo*, an occasion for immediacy of experience, a nonreducible mode of beauty, of contrast and resolution, of order and of ecstasy flowing through and beyond the order. Order, and ecstasy rooted in order: that sounds like the relation between law and love, law and gospel. In these qualities of music there is something more than pleasant and ordered sound, something transmusical. How is one to express this extramusical quality? Often the question is asked of an artist, what is the meaning of this piece of music? And the artist is tempted to reply simply by playing the music again. Is the playing and the listening to the music only a game, the enjoyment of contrast and its resolution? I think not. But, in a time of the breakdown of old myths and symbols, the answer perhaps communicates little that is persuasive. One could speak of a music of the innocence of creation, the music that reaffirms the song of the morning stars at the beginning of creation. One could speak of the music of the Fall, the music that expresses a sense, a metaphysical sense, of humanity's alienation from the innocence of creation. One could speak of the music of redemption, the music of the third movement of Stravinsky's *Symphony of Psalms*, when alienation and tragedy are overcome, yet with the sense also that there always will be alienation and tragedy and suffering. It is not hyperbole to suggest that at times the music of Bob Dylan combines these dimensions, giving utterance to the joy of creation and to the protest of youth against social evil, and also summoning one to participation in "The Times, They Are A-Changing." The same dimensions appear in the martial music of the civil rights movement: "We Shall Overcome."

The music that rouses to a new sense of promise and to new resolve serves as a judgment upon the actualities of the present and at the same time as a contemplation, a harbinger, of future fulfillment. It can also make one "calm of mind, all passion spent" if it is the music that says "hallowed be thy name, thy kingdom come." The sense of frustration is the sense that humanity is made for fulfillment, that alienation, and the separation of person from person, the sad music of inhumanity of one to another, is a shadow that reminds us of the sun and of a Presence that both judges and sustains. With a special sense of immediacy and inwardness, authentic music redefines, illumines, refreshes, orders our experience. It is not escape from reality; it is rather the rediscovery of a center of meaning and power, of a center that is a symptom and sign of faith—ultimately not a human achievement but a gift of grace. In short, the authentic music of high seriousness elicits what cannot be put into words. It is a "joyful creation" that enables us to sing without words, "Holy, Holy, Holy, is the Lord who was and is and is to come."

Time and History

History is made by groups. Groups form parties, industries, trade associations, patriotic associations, sit-in demonstrations, colleges, foundations. The groups to which we belong largely determine the quality and the relevance of our sensitivities and commitments in the face of the changing community. Certain groups to which we belong may serve to diffuse identity, or to draw us merely into the realm of the undifferentiated, of the interchangeable person. Other groups may rigidify and foreclose our sensitivities and commitments. Other groups define and elicit a wider and deeper kind of sharing of perspectives and commitment.

Respecting this associational dimension of human existence, we may say *by their groups shall you know them*. It is through group participation that sensitivity and commitment to values are given institutional expression. It is through groups that social power is organized. It is through groups that community needs are brought to the focus that affects public policy. It is through groups that the cultural atmosphere of a community and a nation is created.

—"By Their Groups Shall You Know Them,"
James Luther Adams, 1969

Taking Time Seriously

This is Adams's classic, mid-life autobiographical essay, describing his lifetime quest for a faith and a philosophy that "take time seriously"—neither escaping into a mystical eternity nor an interior "spirituality," but shaping personal vocation and "making history rather than being pushed around by it." Here he recounts a decisive religious experience of his young adulthood occasioned by singing Bach's Mass in B minor. *This essay was a contribution to* The Christian Century's *end of the decade series, "How My Mind Has Changed." It was published in September 1939, just as the global crisis that Adams had brooded over was erupting in war.*—GKB

I

My earliest recollection goes back to the year 1906 when I was four years old. Our family was kneeling in prayer, all of us burying our heads in pillows. We could scarcely breathe, for our farmhouse was in the path of one of the worst dust storms of a decade in the Pacific Northwest, and we were praying for relief. A few minutes before, blinded by the dust, I had lost my way in the farmyard, and on rejoining the family circle my prayer may well have been one of thanksgiving for having found the path to the house as well as of petition for the quieting of the wind. I was told much later that my father, a Baptist country preacher of premillinarian persuasion, prayed then and there for the Second Coming.

At one time my father was what might be called a circuit rider and I can remember riding behind him on horseback on some of his trips. Later on, I used to take my violin along to accompany the hymn singing.

My father was as otherworldly as the head of a family could possibly be. Very often he would tell us after family prayers before retiring at night that we might not see each other again on this earth. Christ might come before the morning and we should all meet him in the air. He interpreted the World War as evidence of the approaching end of the present "dispensation." Later on, after he had joined the Plymouth Brethren, he refused on religious principle to vote. He gave up his life insurance policy because he felt it betrayed a lack of faith in God. When he was employed by the American Railway Express Company he refused to join the union on the ground that it was a worldly organization with worldly aims. Indeed, he had taken up railway work because of his decision to follow St. Paul's example and refuse to accept wages for preaching the gospel. In short, my father was a man of principle.

By the age of eleven I knew the whole plan of salvation according to the Scofield Reference Bible, and I testified for it in season and out. I even preached on the street and at the Salvation Army during my earlier years in college. The break came before I left college, but I did not give up religion. I simply changed my attitude: I decided that it was my mission to attack religion in season and out. I became a "campus radical" and joined with some other quondam fundamentalists to publish an undergraduate freelance sheet which we smugly called the *Angel's Revolt*. My new law was in the scientific humanism of John Deitrich and my new prophecy was in the anti-Rotarianism of H. L. Mencken.

One of the great surprises of my life came at the end of my senior year in college. I had been taking a course in public speaking and all my speeches had been vicious attacks on religion as I knew it—at least, they had been as vicious as I could make them. Then the shock came one day when on leaving the classroom I happened to say quite casually to the professor that I did not know what I was going to do after graduation. I was already profitably engaged in business, but I was thoroughly discontented. The professor replied in a flash, "You don't know what you are going to do? Why I have known for months. Come around and talk to me some day." And then, right there in the presence of my enemies, the fundamentalists, he smote me. "There is no possible doubt about it," he said. "You are going to be a preacher!" Later, I went by night, like Nicodemus, to question this strange counselor, Professor Frank Rarig. Within six weeks the arrangements were complete. I was to attend Harvard Divinity School.

II

The changes that have taken place in me since then have been changes largely characterized by a slow process of deprovincialization, and yet by a process that has found its frame of reference for the most part in the catholic tradition of Christianity. The thread of continuity running through these changes has been an interest in history. Hence the French proverb that the more human nature changes the more it remains the same, may find some illustration in my own thinking. After all, the expectation of the Second Coming "when time shall be no more" involved at least an otherworldly, negative interest in history. The major change (aside from a difference in attitude toward science and toward the kind of authority the Bible possesses) centers around a change of attitude toward, rather than a diminution of interest in, time. Whereas in my youth I felt myself to be a stranger in time, a pilgrim on a foreign strand, now (largely under the influence of Dewey, Whitehead, Tillich, and the Bible) I believe time itself to be of the essence of both God and human being. Whereas formerly I thought of salvation as an escape of the elect from time, I now envisage it as taking place in community and in time, whether here, or hereafter.

III

At the beginning of this decade, I was a disciple of Irving Babbitt, the leader of the movement known as literary humanism. As I look back on this phase of development, it seems to me that there was little at variance between what I took from Babbitt and what I had gained from the theological and historical disciples of the divinity school. Babbitt (along with Paul Elmer More) did for me what he did for hundreds of others. He made the religious ideas of Plato, the Buddha, and Jesus, as well as Christian theology, come alive. He led us back to fundamental ideas, but by a path that seemed new.

Scientific humanism had stressed a faith in education and in progress through science. At the same time it was, when consistent, purely relativistic in its ethics. Literary humanism, to my mind, had a more realistic conception of human nature: It envisaged the central problem of civilization as that of ethical standards and, without being obscurantist, it stressed the necessity of something like conversion, of a change in the will whereby a person would develop an inner ethical control and work toward a richly human, universal norm. Through Babbitt's stress on these ideas I came to understand and value Greek and Chinese humanism, the Christian doctrine of sin and grace, and the Christian emphasis on conversion and humility. I also thus acquired a skepticism of the romantic liberal conception of human nature which was later to be so severely scrutinized by "realistic theology."

Yet literary humanism, despite its challenging sense of the past, did not possess a dynamic conception of history. The meaning of history tended to be localized more in the individual than in society. This was, to be sure, a needed emphasis at a time when humanitarianism was equated with Christianity by many of the "social gospelers," and with religion by scientific humanists. But, with the reading of Karl Marx and a study of the Anglo-catholic view of the church and its role in society, I began to look upon literary humanism as more satisfactory as an individual psychology of self-culture than as a social and institutional psychology. Literary humanism did not, except in the schools, elicit participation in the process by which a more just social order and even a humanistic education are to be achieved.

Moreover, the humanistic interpretations of sin and grace and humility were truncated. As I indicated in my long critique of literary humanism, which appeared in *Hound and Horn* in 1932, these interpretations seemed to me to be only humanistic parodies of Christian theology. Humanism envisaged them in too narrow a frame of reference. It reckoned without its host "our neighbor the universe." Both scientific and literary humanism had done what Millet did when he first painted the *Sower*. They and he alike left no room on the canvas for the field into which the sower was casting his seed. Like the Millet of the second (and better known) painting, I felt that the man should be placed in a larger setting, so that there might be two principles rather than one: the man *and* the earth upon which he is dependent for the growth of the seed.

It was only later that the New Testament idea concerning the seed growing of itself was to be impressed upon me by Rudolf Otto. At that time, Henry Nelson Wieman's definition of God provided a great stimulus. Religion, I came to believe, requires the declarative as well as the imperative mood. It has to do with facts as well as with hopes and demands, facts about human beings, especially about the resources upon which we are dependent for growth and re-creation. I began to appreciate again certain aspects of the Christian doctrines of creation and redemption. Humanism, in eschewing metaphysics, presupposed an unexamined metaphysics, and I decided that an unexamined metaphysics was not worth having.

My gratitude to Irving Babbit has increased with the years and will probably continue to increase; indeed I have tried to give expression to it in my contribution to the volume in honor of Babbitt published by some of his students. Nevertheless, I was constrained to go beyond humanism, both scientific and literary. My desire was to find a metaphysics in addition to ethical standards and a meaning in history which would involve them both.

IV

At this time two significant changes took place. One of those changes was brought about through my work as a minister in the liberal church. The other was introduced through my reading of Baron Friedrich von Hügel. But before speaking of these developments, I should like to repeal reticence still further by referring to a personal experience.

At the beginning of this decade I was a graduate student of philosophy and comparative literature at Harvard. During this period I became a member of the Harvard Glee Club. Nathan Söderblom has remarked that Bach's *St. Matthew Passion* music should be called the fifth evangelist. So was Bach for me. One night after singing with the club in the *Mass in B Minor* under Serge Koussevitzky at Symphony Hall in Boston, a renewed conviction came over me that here in the mass, beginning with the *Kyrie* and proceeding through the *Crucifixus* to the *Agnus Dei* and *Done nobis pacem*, all that was essential in the human and the divine was expressed. My love of the music awakened in me a profound sense of gratitude to Bach for having displayed as through a prism and in a way that was irresistible for me, the essence of Christianity.

I realize now that this was only the culmination of my *preparatio evangelica*. For suddenly I wondered if I had a right even to enjoy what Bach had given me. I wondered if I was not a spiritual parasite, one who was willing to trade on the costly spiritual heritage of Christianity, but who was perhaps doing very little to keep that spirit alive. In the language of Kierkegaard, I was forced out of the spectator into the "existential" attitude. This experience as such was, to be sure, not a new one: It was simply a more decisive one. I could now see what Nietzsche meant when, in speaking of the *Passion* music, he said, "Whoever has wholly forgotten Christianity will hear it there again."

V

As an active minister (which I had been from the time of my graduation from Harvard Divinity School in 1927), I began to feel an increasing uneasiness about religious liberalism. It appeared to me to represent a cultural lag, the tail end of the laissez-faire philosophy of the nineteenth century. Its competitive character and its atomistic individualism forced upon me the question of what the theological method of liberalism is and should be, and also of what its religious content actually is. Reinhold Niebuhr, Walter Marshall Horton, and John Bennett had their share in pointing up these questions, if not in raising them. Especially influential at that time was T. S. Eliot's criticism of Babbitt's cosmopolitanism and the strictures of Hermenlink and Otto upon so-called universal religion.

Through these writers as well as through personal experience I came to see that religion lives not only by means of universally valid *ideas*, but also through the warmer, more concrete, historical tradition that possesses its sense of community, it prophets and its "acts" of the apostles, its liturgy and literature, its peculiar language and disciplines. "The spirit killeth, the letter giveth life." Not that I doubted the validity of the principle of disciplined freedom. Rather the question was:

Is there a liberal church, or are there only aggregates of individuals, each claiming to search the truth—as though none had yet been found? Despite my (still existing) conviction that the empirical method is the proper one for theology, anglo-catholicism and Barthianism with their respective emphases on common faith and "church theology" served as a challenge.

These questions were the source of great distress to me. I even contemplated giving up the ministry and going into teaching. Indeed, I did later become a full-time instructor in English at Boston University, continuing the while my work as a minister.

Some of the younger Unitarian ministers in New England had organized themselves into a study group for the purpose of working out together a critique of liberalism and also of searching for a remedy. Over a period of years this group (later to be known as the Greenfield Group) read, discussed, and wrote papers on the outstanding theologians of the twentieth century as well as on some of the earlier ones, both Roman Catholic and Protestant. They hammered out together a "church theology" that would enable them as liberals to restate in modern terms the Christian doctrines of God and the human being, of sin and grace, and of the church. Pursuing the implications of their group method, they attempted to set forward the principle disciplines that these doctrines seemed to demand. Nor did they confine their attention to the harmless concerns of academic theology. The necessity of carrying their conclusions over into the work of the church and a year spent studying books like Troeltsch's *Social Teachings of the Christian Churches* helped us, as F. R. Barry would say, to make our Christianity relevant. But many of us felt that we had much to do yet before we learned to take contemporary history seriously.

Although von Hügel did not meet this need for orientation in time, his influence upon me and certain other Unitarian ministers in the Greenfield Group was profound. My own interest in von Hügel I owe, like many another fruit-bearing seed, to Dean Willard Sperry of Harvard Divinity School. Von Hügel's philosophy of critical realism, his emphasis on the role of the body, history, and institutions in religion, his attack (along with Maritain's) on the "pure spirituality" of unhistorical, noninstitutional, nonincarnational religion became determinative for my conception of religion. Much of this side of von Hügel was the more impressive because of the way in which he showed how James Martineau, a Unitarian theologian, had espoused similar views. Through reading von Hügel's *Letters to a Niece* I found a new reality in the devotional life, especially because of his insistence that there should remain a tension between the sacred and the secular, and between Hebraism, Hellenism, and science.

I went on from von Hügel to the reading of certain other spiritual directors of history, and especially of St. Francis of Sales. Several groups of Unitarian ministers at about this time were developing cooperatively certain disciplines for the devotional life. One of our groups (the Brothers of the Way), suspicious of the sort of devotions that aim at a cloistered virtue, included within its disciplines weekly visits of mercy to the needy, a "general" discipline of active participation in some secular organization of socially prophetic significance, and an annual retreat where we participated in discussions of social issues and in the sacraments of silence and of the Lord's Supper.

A sense for the ontological, the historical, and the institutional elements in Christianity was by now deeply formed. Still I only vaguely apprehended the relation of all these things to the history that was in the making. This statement seems to me accurate despite the fact that I had been actively involved in strikes (a minister could not live in Salem, Massachusetts, without having something to do with strikes), despite the fact that I knew something about the lot of the laborer by having worked for six years on the railroad, and despite the fact that one of our groups of Unitarian ministers had for a period used St. Francis of Sales and Karl Marx for daily devotional reading. I was not yet taking time seriously. Von Hügel, like Babbitt, had increased in me a sense of the past which gave perspective to immediate interests, but he had no theology for social salvation.

VII

In 1935 and 1936 I spent almost a year abroad in preparation for coming to teach at the Meadville Theological

School in Chicago. Because of my interest in the liturgical movement, I devoted a portion of my time to visiting Benedictine monasteries. But I spent the greater part of the year attending lectures in philosophy and theology in French and Swiss universities. I also became familiar with the writings of a French Protestant religious socialist, André Philip, a professor of law in Lyons and a member of the Chamber of Deputies.

Pursuing still further my interest in the devotional life, I secured through the good offices of Catholic friends in America a spiritual director at the famous seminary of Saint Sulpice in Paris. Two hours a week for a period of three months with one of the finest spirits I have known will not be forgotten. Here I came to know a man for whom the devotional life was far more than discipline. It was a growing in the grace and knowledge of Christ. He did for me what I should have expected from a Protestant: he acquainted me with a living Christ. Yet the Christ he made vivid for me was not the harbinger of the Kingdom, but rather the obedient servant of God in the inner life and in the personal virtues.

On leaving France I went to live with an old Harvard friend, Peter Brunner, who was a professor of theology in a Confessional Front theological school and who had just been released from a concentration camp. Through his aid I became acquainted with Confessional Church leaders in the various sections of Germany. I saw with my own eyes what I had previously not seen even in print. I accompanied one young minister just out of concentration camp on a preaching tour, and I heard him speak out against the government, mincing no words, knowing that very often, the secret police were in his audience.

I soon learned, of course, that these Confessional people have little interest in strictly social and political questions, that they are scarcely aware of the fact that their present plight is tied in with the breakdown of capitalism. But I learned at first hand what it means when we say that the struggle in our world is between paganism and Christianity, between nationalism and Christianity. I talked not only with Martin Niemöller, but also with his enemies and with leaders in the German Christian and pagan movements. I learned what the existential attitude is in a situation where the options are living options. By hearing it read in the homes of the persecuted, I learned again how the Bible may be more than something to be read as great literature. I learned the meaning of decision and commitment.

Then I went to visit Rudolf Otto, who was in retirement and whom I had the good fortune to see for an hour or two a day throughout the summer. The struggle of the church was never for long out of our conversation. But more important for me were the discussions of his last, and greatest, book, *The Kingdom of God and the Son of Man*. In his interpretation of Jesus I saw again the man who took time seriously: "The kingdom of heaven is at hand." Already it has partially entered into time, it grows of itself by the power of God (here again was the seed growing of itself), it demands repentance, it is an earnest of the sovereignty of God. It is a mystery. Yet the struggle between the divine and the demonic is evident to all who can read the signs of the times.

VIII

Scarcely a better preparation than the reading of André Phillip and the time spent with Otto and among the Confessional Church leaders could have been given me for becoming acquainted subsequently in 1936 and again in 1938 with another group, certain students and admirers of Paul Tillich. I had first become familiar with Tillich's point of view when I was in Germany in 1927. For his appreciation of his use of the voluntarist tradition beginning with Duns Scotus and coming down through Jakob Böhme and later Friedrich Schelling, I had been prepared also by previous acquaintance with the writings of Kurt Leese of Hamburg.

In Tillich's writings I now found a binding together of many of the more significant things that had attracted me in the preceding decade. In his theology I was confronted by a prophetic restatement of the Kingdom, of the divine and the demonic, of time being fulfilled, of sin and grace, all interpreted in the light of the voluntaristic tradition that I had earlier approached through pragmatism as well as through literary humanism. And, what is more important for me, they were interpreted also in relation to the social (and antisocial) realities that

constitute present-day history: self-sufficient nationalism, fascism, communism, capitalism, Bible Protestantism, Roman Catholicism, estheticism, intellectualism on
the side of virtual resistance to the grace of God acting
in history, and a religious socialism thenomously aware
of the dialectical nature of God, human being, and history on the other side.

There is much in Tillich that still remains for me
obscure and, where understood, unacceptable. His view
of Christ as the center of history and his reading of his
own philosophy of religion into Reformation theology
are to me unconvincing. Yet, it seems to me that American theologians have much to gain from acquiring a
greater familiarity with his work, much of which remains
untranslated. In Tillich's view of the dialectical nature
of reality, of revelation, of God, of the Kingdom, of human nature and history, I find an interpretation and an
application of Christian doctrine which are far more
relevant to the social and divine forces that determine
the destiny of humanity than in any other theologian I
happen to know about. Here, if ever, is a theologian who
takes time seriously. This aspect of his thought comes
best into relief when he is contrasted with Barth. Indeed, Tillich has made the most penetrating criticism
of so-called dialectical theology that has yet appeared,
namely, that it is not in truth dialectical.

One who takes time seriously, however, must do more
than talk about it. He must learn somehow to take time
by the forelock. He must learn to act as a Christian and

as a citizen through socially effective institution, to do what E. C. Lindeman has called the humdrum work of democracy. I for one now believe that every Christian should be actively and persistently engaged in the work of at least one secular organization that is exercising a positive influence for the sake of peace and justice against the forces of hate and greed. But this is, of course, not enough.

The question is whether the churches as corporate bodies can learn to take contemporary history seriously, whether Christianity will act in time, whether it will not as at the beginning be betrayed in its critical moment by those who sit at its table. The danger is, as Stanley Jones has recently warned us, that the church will be more interested in itself than in the Kingdom. Otto Dibelius once inadvertently wrote of the twentieth century as the "century of the church." What has happened since that phrase was coined lends to it an ironic and ominous overtone. This is indeed the century of the church. It is the century in which the church will have to decide unequivocally whether it means business, whether it will play a constructive role in the dynamic process that makes history meaningful. It will have to come to grips with pacifism, nationalism, and capitalism.

This then, is the change that the decade has wrought in me. Christianity is no longer an optional luxury for me. Salvation does not come through worship and prayer alone, nor through private virtues that camouflage public indolence. Time and history are fraught with judgment and fulfillment. *We* are in the valley of decision. But there is reason for hope, for God will make all his mountains a way.

The Prophethood
of All Believers

Adams has often contrasted the priestly and the prophetic functions of religion. The priest invokes the divine presence for blessing and seeks to bring spiritual healing. The prophet invokes divine judgment upon injustice and seeks radical spiritual and social transformation. Although he characteristically accents the prophetic function in religion, Adams holds the priestly element to be complementary and equally important. He also insists that these roles pertain not only to the ordained clergy, but also to "the people"—the laity. Thus Adams took Martin Luther's principle, "the priesthood of all believers," and radically extended it to "the prophethood of all believers." The idea is deeply rooted in the Bible; even Moses said, "Would that all the Lord's people were prophets, and that the Lord would put his spirit upon them" (Numbers 11:29). This essay was originally published in 1947.—GKB

One of the more vivid recollections of my youth in a fundamentalist group is the memory of their eager interest in the prophecies of the Bible. These prophecies were believed to encompass almost the entire range of human history. One all-embracing "prophetic" image that looms in my mind is that of an immense chart that adorned the wall of the church auditorium.

This chart depicted the pivotal events of creation and redemption, beginning with the original chaos and proceeding through the six days of creation, the first day of rest, the fall, the various dispensations of Old Testament history on down to the annunciation, the incarnation, the crucifixion, and the resurrection and thence on to the Second Coming of Christ, the Battle of Armageddon, the seven years of tribulation, the thousand-year reign of Christ, the chaining of Satan in hell, the last judgment before the great white throne, and the eternal peace and unquiet of the respective final destinations of all human souls. In short, the epochs of "salvation history" were set forth as "by prophet bards foretold."

Religious liberals are accustomed to emphasize the prophetic task of the church. But we have long ago abandoned the whole idea of predicting the future by means of interpreting the biblical prophecies. In conformity with the findings of modern historical research, we have held that prediction is a secondary and even an unimportant aspect of Old Testament prophecy. Accordingly, we say that the prophets were primarily forthtellers and not foretellers; they proclaimed the action of God in history; they disclosed the meaning of history. We see the prophet as one who stands at the edge of a community's experience and tradition, under the Great Taskmaster's eye, viewing human life from a piercing perspective and bringing an imperative sense of the perennial and inescapable struggle of good against evil, of justice against injustice. In the name of the Holy One the prophet shakes us out of our pride and calls for a change of heart and mind and action. With fear and trembling the prophet announces crisis and demands ethical decision here and now.

This function of prophecy is well symbolized by a visual metaphor that is said to appear in a church in Toronto. On the altar in this church there stands a large crucifix on which the figure at first seems to be an importunate question mark, the prophetic question mark that stands over humanity's ways that are not the ways of truth and right. It is the question mark that we would often like to liquidate, for it reminds us of the death-dealing effect of our egotism and our "virtue."

But we fall far short of understanding the full nature of prophecy (and of the prophetic task of the church) if we think of the prophets merely as critics dealing with religious and ethical generalities. In the great ages of prophecy the prophets (whether inside or outside the churches) have been foretellers as well as forthtellers. They have been predicters—proclaimers of doom and judgment, heralds of new fulfillment. They have attempted to interpret the signs of the times and to see into the future. They have stood not only at the edge of their own culture but also before the imminent shape of new and better things to come. At times of impending change and decision, they have seen the crisis as the crisis of an age; they have felt called to foresee the coming of a new epoch. That is, they have been "epochal thinkers." Wherever you find a prophet of world-historical significance you find a foreteller, and you find "epochal thinking." By this kind of prophecy the signs of the times are interpreted as parts of a pattern, of an old pattern in the structure of the society which is passing away or of a new pattern of life which is coming into being. Jeremiah and Isaiah, Jesus and Paul, Augustine and Joachim of Fiore were all epochal thinkers in this sense; they saw themselves as standing between the times, between the epochs.

Prophetic prediction and epochal thinking have played an equally significant role in modern times also. The Radical Reformation of the sixteenth century, the heralds of the Renaissance, the mystical and radically democratic sects of the seventeenth century, the democratic revolutionists of the eighteenth century (including the founders of our own nation), the religious liberals of the same period, evolutionists and scientists, and the proponents of the Social Gospel in the nineteenth century—all were prophet bards foretelling, and struggling for, a new epoch.

Not all of these prophets have appeared within the churches. Indeed, some of the most influential of the epochal thinkers in the nineteenth century prophesied against "religion" as inextricably bound up with the passing epoch and as marked for elimination. Karl Marx, for example, in his attempt to interpret the signs of the times, predicted the end of the age of the bourgeoisie and the advent of a new epoch, the real beginning of history in the age of the classless society. He tried to support this prophecy by means of a "science" of society. The influence of Marx even upon non-Marxist thinking has been a profound one, for he has given to the masses a new concern for the "trend" of history and for epochal thinking. Even the proponents of "free enterprise" (the defenders of an earlier progressivist epochal thinking) have been constrained to defend their outlook in terms of prediction and of a theory of the inexhaustibility and viability of the present age. Friedrich Nietzsche, the great critic of Christian "slave morality" and of Prussianism, demanded, like Marx, that the scientist become a philosopher of culture and of history, a demand that many a scientist in the new atomic age is now beginning to recognize; and he predicted (with shrewd accuracy) the present nihilism of European culture as the consequence of the loss of spiritual vitality. He also heralded the coming of a new human. "Man is something that shall be surpassed." August Comte, an even more influential epochal thinker, took up the theme of the coming "third era" (proclaimed in varying ways before him by Joachim and Lessing and Hegel and Marx) and heralded the "third era" of science, the era that was to replace the ages of theology and metaphysics. Under his influence and under similar influences many social scientists have come to hold that their work should include prediction. Indeed, many would say that the ideal of science is to acquire the sort of knowledge that will provide a basis for prediction. So the social scientists (or at least some of them) have become interpreters of the signs of the times, attempting to discriminate the trends of the time and to describe our present position in the changing epoch. Edward Alsworth Ross of the University of Wisconsin, in considering the prophetic elements in contemporary sociology, has recently asserted, "Insight into the future is, in fact, the 'acid test' of our understanding. . . . From the days of Comte our slogan has been *Voir pour prévoir,* i.e., see in order to foresee."

It is not an exaggeration to say that the "anti-Christian" critics of our culture (such critics as Marx, Nietzsche, and Comte) have done more than the churchpeople to revive prophetism as prediction and as epochal thinking. As forthtellers (that is, as interpreters of the ultimate meaning of life) they could learn much about the religious character of true prophetism, but as foretellers and as epochal thinkers they cannot be ignored. We live in a world of change and as religious liberals we have the obligation to confront the problems posed by our social economy, the problems of depression and unemployment and insecurity which have become characteristic of the present phase of that economy. Only those who have a priestly attachment to the status quo (which moves whether we like it or not) will try to persuade us that we are living in a former stage of our epoch or that new occasions do not teach new duties. This sort of attachment produces the false prophets who say, "Ye shall have peace at this time." They say "unto everyone that walketh after the imagination of his own heart, 'No evil shall come upon you.'"

This spirit of false prophecy has been plainly exhibited of late in the journals that have been commending President Truman for his refusal to predict the future in his address to Congress on the state of the nation (even though he had been charged by Congress to do that very thing). To be sure, they do not say that business people should eschew foresight and planning for the future; but they do give the impression that they believe that national history should simply take its course without benefit of foresight. They seem now to say, "No evil shall come upon you." Then when it is too late to prevent a catastrophe, will they say the catastrophe was not our fault, or that it could not have been prevented even if we had tried? It is no wonder that the United States is rapidly regaining its 1929 reputation of being a "bad economic neighbor."

When we speak of prophecy, of prediction, of epochal thinking, a host of questions comes immediately to mind. Can one predict with accuracy what will happen to the entire economy? Do we know enough to make our predictions more than wild guesses? Should we not confine ourselves to piecemeal predictions? Is it not fanciful and even dangerous to talk about new epochs? Does this talk not lead to utopianism and irresponsible tinkering and experimenting? How does one choose from among the predicters? And how can religious belief contribute to prophetic criticism anyway? These questions demand and deserve answers.

But whatever the answers may be, this much we can say. A church that does not concern itself with the struggle in history for human decency and justice, a church that does not show concern for the shape of things to come, a church that does not attempt to interpret the signs of the times, is not a prophetic church. We have long held to the idea of the *priesthood* of all believers, the idea that all believers have direct access to the ultimate resources of the religious life and that every believer has the responsibility of achieving an explicit faith for free persons. As an element of the radical laicism we need also a firm belief in the *prophethood* of all believers. The prophetic liberal church is not a church in which the prophetic function is assigned merely to the few. The prophetic liberal church is the church in which persons think and work together to interpret the signs of the times in the light of their faith, to make explicit through discussion the epochal thinking that the times demand. The prophetic liberal church is the church in which all members share the common responsibility to attempt to foresee the consequences of human behavior (both individual and institutional), with the intention of making history in place of merely being pushed around by it. Only through the prophetism of all believers can we together foresee doom and mend our common ways.

Hope is a virtue, but only when it is accompanied by prediction and by the daring venture of new decision, only where the prophethood of all believers creates epochal thinking. If this foresight and this epochal thinking do not emerge from the churches, they will have to come from outside the churches. Humanity can surpass itself. Do we as religious liberals have access to the religious resources for this surpassing of the present? If not, the time will come when others will have to say to us what Henry IV said to the tardy Crillon after victory had been won, "Hang yourself, brave Crillon! We fought at Arques, and you were not there."

The Evolution of
My Social Concern

Social-ethical concerns—racism, nationalism, sexism, war, economic exploitation—play a prominent role in Adams's thought. Adams does not propose "solutions" to these massive problems, but forcefully asserts that we must engage in the struggle against them. We must learn from our experiences and be faithful to our moral commitments. Here Adams reports his encounters with people, movements, and ideas that shaped his social concerns.—GKB

I was reared in a Plymouth Brethren home where the name of Darby was a household word and where the Scofield Reference Bible, with its *heilsgeschichtliche* footnotes on the dispensations was the daily food. Indeed the food at table always followed the spiritual repast of the Bible-reading. In accord with Scofield's footnotes, my father's constant attention was devoted to interpreting apocalyptically the signs of the times. This whole apparatus, and even the interest in the Bible, disappeared from my consciousness for a time when evolutionary humanism and then classical humanism (under Irving Babbitt) took their place.

Awakening Social Conscience

Considering the early training, I find it no accident that following upon my student years at Harvard in theology my experiences of Nazism in Germany during the summer of 1927 became crucial for me. However, they did not assume full significance in my consciousness until the middle thirties when I spent some months in the so-called "underground" movement of the Confessing Church in Germany. Meanwhile, I had resumed graduate studies at Harvard. These were years in which my acquired religious liberalism came under the scrutiny that we associate with that period in American Protestantism. The awareness of the thinness of its theology was in part stimulated by the Whiteheadean concern for metaphysics, by Irving Babbitt's vigorous attack upon Romantic conceptions of human nature, and by von Hügel's emphasis upon the theological, the historical, the institutional, and the devotional elements in Christianity. The depression and the early Roosevelt years, along with a markedly unideological interest in the writings of Marx, an increasing interest in the problems of unemployment and of the labor movement, participation as a minister in the activities incident to the great textile strike in Salem, Massachusetts—all these things conspired to develop a social concern, both theoretical and practical, which had previously been relatively peripheral. At the same time, the development of the fissiparous individualism and the unprophetic character of the conventional middle-class, humanitarian religious liberalism served to increase my concern for the nature and mission of the church and especially for the *ecclesiola in ecclesia* as indispensable for the achievement of significant and costing consensus relevant to the historical situation.

Some of us Unitarian ministers initiated a study group just before I went to Germany in 1927. The group undertook a vigorous year-round discipline of reading, discussion and the writing of papers. We collectively studied major literature of the time in the fields of theology, Bible, historical theology, social philosophy, art, liturgy, prayer, ever seeking consensus and seeking common disciplines whereby we could implement consensus in the church and the community. During one entire summer, for example, we read thoroughly and discussed at length Troeltsch's *Social Teaching of the Christian Churches*. Reinhold Niebuhr and Karl Mannheim, of course, figured largely in our study. Such groups have increased through the years, and they continue in several parts of the country. I speak of this group discipline here, because in my conviction the concern for group participation and group responsibility became increasingly crucial in the quest for identity.

Studies in Europe

These multiple concerns were brought to a convergence by my second, more prolonged visit to Europe, a year of study of theology, of prayer and liturgy, of fascism and its persecution of the churches. During a period of several months at the Sorbonne, also at the Protestant theological faculty, and at the Catholic Institute, I lived in the home of a retired professor of the Sorbonne. Another paying guest in this home was a right-wing nationalist student. Many an hour we spent arguing the issues between democracy and fascism. I soon became aware of the fact that he would shoot me down in cold blood if his wave of the future came to flood tide. I cannot enter here into detail about the experiences of those days. Listening to lectures daily at the hands of a liberal theologian, of an orthodox Calvinist, and of the principle Parisian Barthian—none of them making any analytic effort to interpret the signs of the times, signs that were the chief interest of the secularists—the Fascists and the Marxists. Meanwhile, I was also under the tutelage of an eminent Jesuit spiritual director at the Roman Catholic Seminary of Saint-Sulpice. Each week I posed my questions on prayer, and the following week he answered them. But I always felt the gap between the cultivation of mental prayer and the bludgeonings of a period of history that was swiftly moving into the storms of our time. I recall an experience not dissimilar to the one of 1927 in Nuremberg. Early one morning I went to the Pantheon to watch the formation of a United Front parade. When I began to move, I could not get out of the jam. Willy nilly I marched; no escape was possible. Every cross street was filled with crowds of people, obstructed also by a police cordon. For two hours I marched, pushed along as if I had been seized by the elbows and at every moment seeing people give the Communist salute from the windows of the buildings. On the day when Hitler marched into the Rhineland, I was in the home of Edgar Ansel Mowrer. We stayed up all night.

It is perhaps not surprising that soon after this in Geneva I adopted the counsel of the young Visser 't Hooft. "You are to study in the German universities? I hope that is not all! I am going to give you the advice that I constantly give to churchmen going to Germany. But none of them takes my advice. I say you should get into the underground of the Confessing Churches and learn the meaning of the Synod of Barmen."

I took his advice, though I also attended the lectures of Bultmann and Heiler, of Jaspers and Barth and Brunner, of Heim and even of Wilhelm Hauer, the founder of the German Faith Movement. I cannot here narrate the melodramatic experiences of the underground, largely in company with or under the auspices of a former Harvard friend, Peter Brunner, who had served time in the Dachau Concentration Camp and who is now Professor of Theology at Heidelberg. For several months, during an interim, I spent two or more hours a day with the retired Rudolf Otto at Marburg, at the same time taking the lectures of Bultmann and others in the University. In view of my connections with leaders in the Confessing Church, Rudolf Otto saw to it that I should get acquainted with German Christians, Nazis among the clergy whom he deemed to be insane.

It is extremely difficult to pass over a description of the maelstrom of this whole experience in Germany, an experience that brought fearful encounter with the police and even a frightening encounter two years later with the Gestapo. The ostensible charge made by the Gestapo was that I was violating the law by walking in the street with a deposed Jewish teacher and by visiting a synagogue. The word existential came alive in these hours of bludgeoned questioning and of high palpitation. It is difficult, I say, to suppress giving an account of incidents in connection with the Nazis, the anti-Nazis, and the hidden underlings. It is even more difficult to determine how to compress into brief statement what all this did for the evolution of my "social concern."

The Contest of Symbols

One way to do this is in terms of the ideological battles, specifically in terms of symbols. The ideological battle, as Schelling would say, was a war of the gods, a war between myths. Here I express indebtedness to Paul Tillich, whose reputation and writing I began to encounter at this time, seeing in him a German counterpart to Reinhold Niebuhr. I wish I could pause here to speak of the lectures of Jaspers and Heidegger and Bultmann. But let me hasten on. As between Bultmann and Otto, I was the more greatly attracted to Otto. The gnostic existentialism of Bultmann, despite his heroic stand against Hitler, did not speak directly to my condition. Like others in the Confessing Church, he possessed only an abstract conception of concreteness and decision with respect to *positive* action in history. Indeed, his aversion to concern for the historical Jesus and his preference for *kerygma* alone seemed to me to be part and parcel of a really inchoate non-historical outlook, despite the frequent admonition of openness to the future. His concern for anthropology to the exclusion of ontology seemed to me to urge the cart without the horse. The increasing criticism of Bultmann today, even among his quondam disciples, insists on a more historical understanding of history, on the resumption of the quest for the historical Jesus, and on the centrality of ontology.

What gave focus to the whole experience in Germany was Rudolf Otto's *The Kingdom of God and the Son of Man.* The conception of the kingdom as more than judgment, as redemptive dynamics, as the seed that grows of itself in struggle against the demonic powers, the Son of Man as suffering servant, the kingdom as both present and future—all of this represented a turning point away from the consistent eschatology of Schweitzer. In the course of studying simultaneously the anti-prophetic organic symbolism of the Nazi myth, I, like everyone else, became more vividly aware than hitherto of the role of myth in religion and culture, but more specifically I became aware of the *types* of symbolism. Later on I was to realize the ontological significance of myth, particularly at the hands of Schelling, Tillich, and Heidegger.

Later on, too, I was to see the anthropological significance of symbolism—the view that language is a decisive medium for the expression of the freedom of man.
But at the time I was particularly frustrated by the pietistic, individualistic symbolism of Kierkegaard and of
American individualism. Heinrich Frick of Marburg
(whom I saw a great deal) suggested in his *Vergleichende
Religionswissenschaft* [Science of Comparative Religion]
a distinction between symbols drawn from history—
dynamic symbols oriented to time—and symbols drawn
from nature—static symbols oriented to space. The per-
tinence of dynamic symbolism had earlier been impressed upon me by the study of Whitehead.

The "Inner Life" or Institutional Life?

But more significant than this sort of typology was the
distinction between symbols that relate the concept of
the Kingdom of God to the inner life or the life of the
individual and that relate the concept of the Kingdom
of God to institutions, that is to the church and to other
institutions. Quite decisive for me was the recognition
of the *political* character of Biblical symbolism. As political, this symbolism, particularly in the Old Testament,
expressed the sovereignty of God over all life, including the institutional structures. From this time on I saw,
with the aid of Troeltsch, the narrowing of Christian
obligation which in Lutheranism resulted from the two-
kingdom theory—a bifurcation of political symbolism

which makes a dichotomy between the church and culture and thus reduces the tension between them.

In conjunction with a doctrine of vocation oriented not only to daily work, the two-kingdom theory released the eschatological tension and also prevented the doctrine of vocation from including dynamic political obligation. Likewise, the merely interpersonal emphasis on the priesthood of all believers crowded out dynamic functioning of a doctrine of the prophethood of all believers in the face of institutions. In contrast to this institutional orientation of political symbolism, one can readily observe the merely interpersonal orientation of the doctrine of justification by faith or the doctrine of forgiveness. I still offer a prize to students in my classes if they can bring in a report that the Sunday morning Lutheran Hour on TV finds any symbol of the power or the demand of God other than the power and the demand of God to forgive. It is difficult to work out social ethics on the basis of a doctrine of forgiveness. Toward this end, the doctrine must be related to political symbolism. One must emphasize, of course, that both the personal and the institutional belong together in soteriology and in a theological anthropology. To separate them is to violate the sovereignty of God. One sees these two corresponding forms of distortion in Kierkegaard and Marx. Both of these thinkers are unthinkable without the Bible, but in their reduction of ethics exclusively to the personal or to the institutional they are both of them unbiblical. Looking at them, one must say there is nothing so much like a swelling as a hole. Kierkegaard, despite his astute attack upon so-called Christendom, is in Christian circles a form of infidelity to the sovereignty of God over institutions, a sophisticated form of pietism, that is, a form of political and ecclesiastical irresponsibility. In industrial society, pietism tends to support by default the primacy of the economic life over the political.

These considerations underscore the fact that Christians possess almost infinite capacities of dissolving the political symbolism of covenant and kingdom. These forms of dissolution include the reduction of Christian ethics to personalism, systematic theology that has no reference to institutions, psychotherapy that possesses no sociological framework, abstract existentialism that talks about concreteness and decision but does not drive towards actualizing concreteness and decision in the social-historical situation.

Why is it so extremely easy for Christians to become pietistic, in the sense that they see little connection between Christian ethics and structural institutional analysis or between Christian ethics and responsibility for the character and influence of economic and political institutions? One reason for this is the ease with which pietism can appeal for sanction to the Gospels. The first sentence of Troeltsch's *Social Teaching of the Christian Churches* asserts that primitive Christianity was not a social movement. In one of his long essays, *The Social Philosophy of Christianity*, he argues that primitive Christianity had no social philosophy, no articulated theology of social institutions which could provide a critical and positive interpretation of ongoing political and economic institutions. Accordingly, he asserts that early Christianity turned to pagan natural-law doctrine in search of a basis for a social philosophy. I do not need to examine this issue here. I would like to say only that the angelology and the doctrine of Christ the King recently under debate among New Testament scholars offers some challenge to Troeltsch's view. A masterly essay by G. Dehn on the doctrine of the Kingship of Christ appeared in the Barth *Festschrift* of 1936; through the years I have asked my students to familiarize themselves with my translation of this essay. According to this view, the state, for example, is seen to be in a fallen condition and under the aegis of fallen angels; under Christ the King, it and other social forces are in the end to be restored to their essential nature. Thus salvation is for society as well as for the individual. In a recent essay Amos Wilder has suggested that the doctrine of the Kingship of Christ could serve as a new Christian theological basis for Rauschenbusch's Social Gospel. I mention this here only in order to suggest that a continuing problem for Christian ethics is the place of political symbolism. The Nazi movement and the Communist movement have given new urgency to the explication of the political symbolism of the Bible and of later articulations of Christian ethics. It is striking to observe how little the Bultmann school has contributed to contemporary understanding of the political symbolism of the Bible. One must question the adequacy of the Heidiggerian anthropology as a framework for demythologizing the Gospel.

The Crisis of Liberalism

I must now return to consider another aspect of the impact of Nazism upon my social concern. This consideration, if fully set forth, would entail the discussion of the sociology of religion, the philosophy of history, the relations between Christianity and democracy, as well as between Christianity and capitalism and religious socialism. But I must spare you the full rehearsal of those themes. I must be highly selective.

Let me repeal reticence so far as to say that the experience of Nazism induced in me a kind of conversion. I recall a conversation with Karl Jaspers at his home one day in Heidelberg in 1936. I asked him what he deemed to be the contemporary significance of liberal Christianity. He replied with unwonted vehemence, "Religious liberalism has *no* significance. It has *Zwang*—no costing commitment."

He was thinking of the liberals who had become German Christians (Nazis), the while overlooking the impotence and silence of orthodoxy and neo-orthodoxy in the burgeoning period of Nazism, overlooking also the collaboration of the Catholic Center Party and the Vatican with Fascism and Nazism—a collaboration that is now at last receiving candid discussion precisely in Catholic circles in Germany. So Jaspers now offered me some advice. "If I were a young man of liberal preferences today, I would return to the most orthodox branch of my heritage."

Immediately I asked him if he planned to do this himself. He flushed, he blushed, and replied, "I am not making a personal confession. I am giving you a sociological judgment." So spoke the pupil of Max Weber!

I did in those days recover a sense of the centrality of the Bible and of the decisive role in history of both the sacramental and the prophetic elements. I mention only in passing here the influence of Christian art, and especially of Bach, upon me. In addition I pressed upon myself the question, "If Fascism should arise in the States, what in your past performance would constitute a pattern or framework of resistance?" I could give only a feeble answer to the question. My principal political activities had been the reading of the newspaper and voting. I had preached sermons on the depression or in defense of strikers. Occasionally, I uttered protests against censorship in Boston. But I had no adequate conception of citizen participation.

The German Universities Under Nazism

I must now turn to this theme. The German universities, supposedly independent entities, had been fairly easily Nazified. My American acquaintance, Edward

Yarnall Hartshorne, later killed in Marburg when serving as American Military Government director of the universities at Hesse-Nassau, wrote a well documented account of the Nazification of the universities: *The German Universities and National Socialism* (Harvard University Press, 1937). Hitler also liquidated the trade unions. The persecuted Confessional seminary I attended in Elberfeld occupied an abandoned Masonic building. The order was forbidden to hold meetings. Repeatedly I heard anti-Nazis say, If only 1,000 of us in the late twenties had combined in heroic resistance, we could have stopped Hitler. I noticed the stubborn resistance of the Jehovah's Witnesses. I observed also the lack of religious pluralism in a country that had no significant nonconformist movement in the churches. Gradually I came to the conviction that a decisive institution of the viable democratic society is the voluntary association as the medium for the assumption of civic responsibility. Ernst Troeltsch's treatment of voluntarism of associations, his account of the free-church movement and of the associational creativity of the Calvinists began to flood back into memory. I read Max Weber's *Proposal for the Study of Voluntary Association* and his typology of Associations. In his "Proposal" Weber said it had been the genius of the Prussian government to drain off the national energies into Singing Academies, thus diverting attention away from public policy and from civic responsibility. More than Troeltsch, I, the former sectarian (Plymouth Brethren), began to appreciate the role of the aggressive sect in Western history and of its grandchild, the secular voluntary association concerned with public policy.

Voluntary Associations

You will forgive me if I mention here quickly the important ingredients of this development of social concern. I plunged into voluntary associational activity, concerning myself with race relations, civil liberties, housing problems. I joined with newly formed acquaintances in the founding of the Independent Voters of Illinois and I began to learn at first hand about Moral Man and Immoral Society. I traveled to Washington fairly frequently to consult with men like Adlai Stevenson, Jonathan Daniels, and Harold Ickes regarding Chicago politics. At the same time I participated in precinct organization, becoming a doorbell ringer and also consulting with party leaders in back rooms. There is nothing intrinsically unusual about all this. It was only unusual for the Protestant churchman or clergyman. Equally important for me was the new motivation of sociological understanding. The social sciences acquired an existential quality; and increasingly they figured in my thinking, in my associations, and in my courses.

Moreover, this combination of impulses conditioned my historical studies. I turned to the history of the Radical Reformation, to the influence of English Independency and Quakerism on the rise of democracy. From

Bourgeaud I first learned to appreciate the epic sweep of what Whitehead had called the diffusion of opportunity and what I called the dispersion of power, the capacity to participate in social decision. Here with considerable excitement I pursued the theme through modern history—the transfer of radical concern from the Independents and the Levellers to the initiation of rationally devised public agitation and to the initiation of political parties, the spread of this voluntarism into education, and under Methodist leadership the rise of the British labor movement, and so on. In a memorable address by Whitehead before the American Academy of Arts and Sciences in 1941, he spoke of the *gap* between statesmanship and learning, between the process of social coordination and the activities of the vocations and professions. The voluntary association in manifold ways fills in these gaps. Indeed, voluntary association stands between the individual and the state, providing the *opportunity* for achievement and implementation of consensus. It provides, alas, other opportunities, depending on the goals, the constituency, the internal organization of the association. I can mention here the American Medical Association, the name of James Hoffa, or the Board of Trustees of a suburban church in captivity.

Max Weber adumbrated a philosophy of history in terms of his typology of authority—traditionalist, rational legal, and charismatic (relying here in part upon Sohm's *Kirchenrecht)*. Troeltsch offered a typology of religious associations—church, sect, and mystical type—

which became the basis of a philosophy of church history. He has also offered a typology of Christian political theory, arranged according to the degree of reliance upon individual spontaneity or upon the external shaping disciplines. In a general way, all of these philosophies of history may be traced back to Joachim of Flora's theory of the three ages of the church, but more immediately the father of this associational theory of history and its periods is Otto von Gierke. In his magnum opus *Genossenschaftsrecht*, we may recognize a special kind of anthropology. Human beings are associating beings. Their differences may be determined by observing the associations which they form, and by observing the relations between their voluntary and their involuntary associations, the types of participation they give to these associations. Accordingly, Gierke offers a theory of the periodization of Western history from the time of Charlemagne to the eighteenth century, a theory that characterizes the periods in terms of the dominant types of association.

Now the ramifications of associational theory are of course manifold. Maitland and Jenks have traced the history of England in terms of associational theory and practice. Gierke and Fred Carney have shown the great significance of the Calvinist Althius for Protestant theory. Troeltsch and Weber really presuppose Gierke in their works. H. Richard Niebuhr in his neo-Troeltschean work in the *Social Sources of Denominationalism* traces the development of Protestantism in terms of the structure and dynamics of associations.

Two Theses

I would like now at the end to list some theses and some problems. First, some theses very briefly put.

Considering the associational character of human existence, we may say that the social meaning of a theological idea is to be determined in a crucial way by the type of association that it calls for in the minds of the believers. Here we have a special application of the pragmatic theory of meaning. By their groups, their associational fruits, shall ye know them. If the theological or the theological ethical commitment does not issue in associational preference or transformation, it is to this extent not yet clear or meaningful.

Let me give two illustrations. R. B. Braithwaite, the British linguist philosopher, in his book *An Empiricist Approach to Religion* argues that we can determine the meaning of Christianity by observing its consequences for behavior. To be a Christian, he says, means that one is committed to an agapaistic way of life. This view, like Bultmann's openness to the future, is extremely abstract. A Roman Catholic, a Presbyterian, and a Quaker might provisionally agree with Braithwaite. But consider the wide breach of differences they exhibit in their doctrines of the church. We can most quickly determine the meaning of a theological outlook by examining its doctrine of the church.

A second illustration. H. Richard Niebuhr has offered a typology of the relations between Christ and Culture. Here he gives the now familiar rubrics Christ Against Culture, Christ Over Culture, Christ Transforming Culture. The rubrics are scarcely sufficient. Within each of these classifications one can find a considerable variety of associational theories, and in several of the classifications one can find thinkers who would hold very similar associational theories. This fact shows us, on the one hand, that no timeless associational theory may be taken as definitively normative for the Christian. On the other hand, one does not know enough about a particular type of Christian ethos at a given time if one does not know the type of associational arrangements that are preferred. From this perspective, the man from Mars could be misled if he accepted William Adams Brown's claim that the Protestant and the Catholic worship the same God. The man from Mars would do well to look into Sohm's *Kirchenrecht* or into K. Barth's *Christengemeinde und Bürgergemeinde*. At the same time we must say that the Christian ethos can appear in a considerable variety of types of association. To this extent and by this means the Christian ethos is differentiated. It is also differentiated by the types of non-ecclesiastical associations in which the Christian participates. Associational theory contributes to the analysis of meaning by reminding us, "By their groups, shall ye know them." Here the social sciences have their contribution to make by assisting in the study of the types, the structure and dynamics, and the pathology of associations. So much for the pragmatic theory of meaning when applied to associations.

A second thesis I do not need to spell out. Christian vocation extends beyond the job to the church and the community. The means by which the church goes into the world is through the voluntary associations. That is, the responsibility of the Christian is to participate in the associations that define and re-define the actual situation, in the associations that give utterance and body to prophetic protest, and to social change or social stability in associations that provide the opportunity for the Christian and the non-Christian to enter into dialogue and even to achieve a working consensus—in short, in the associations that contribute to the shaping of history. Indeed, it is from these associations that the Christian can carry back to the church experience, significant fact, informed concern, insight demanding interpretations at the hands of the *koinonia*.

Problems of Associations

Now for some problems.

We do not have and we shall probably not be able to get, an adequate study of the history of voluntary associational activity in the various countries, including our own. Arthur Schlesinger, Sr., following the lead of de Tocqueville, has outlined the history of American associations under the title of *A Nation of Joiners*. Great changes with respect to associations have come about in the twentieth century. Many of the changes that were implemented during the nineteenth century within the context of voluntary philanthropic activity have been taken over by the welfare state. There yet remain thousands of associations in the United States. Some of them, like labor unions and the American Medical Association, are scarcely voluntary, and their internal structures exhibit Michel's iron law of oligarchy—the tendency of political organizations to come under the control of a small group of "eager beavers." Doctors who deplore the tight beauracratization despairingly say that in order to break the hierarchy they would have to expend more energy than they can afford—they trained to be doctors and they want to be doctors. Some of the associations provide the opportunity to cross racial and class lines, in order to work for the general welfare. The NAACP, which has lost some of its dynamic, has done much to elevate the status of African Americans and to extend democracy. Many civic associations function to bring about minor reforms, or to serve as watchdogs. On the other hand, many associations serve only special and narrow interests. Pressure groups with enormous budgets enter into collusion in state legislatures and in the national legislature, to promote or obstruct legislation. On the whole, participation in associations concerned with public policy is a middle class phenomenon, and even then in special interest groups. Philanthropic associations in large degree have this middle class constituency. Rev. Robert Cowell of Denver, in his study published in the *Harvard Business School Bulletin* shows that business and professional people, so far from breaking through class and race barriers, more deeply entrench themselves in their own perspectives by participation in philanthropic and service organizations. Like the churches, voluntary associations of this sort shape the society into isolated grooves or channels. Mirra Komarovsky, in her studies of associations in New York City, shows that the average of membership in associations apart from the church is less than one per person. Some indication of the trend in the USA is revealed by the fact that from 1892 to 1948 the percentage of eligible voters who participated in national elections declined from 87 percent to 57 percent—hardly credible. This fact alone reveals the character and the extent of the opportunity for the operation of the political machine. Komarovsky has suggested that nonmembership and nonparticipation in associations concerned with public policy is the criterion for the appearance of the mass man. Add to these facts the structure and power of the American business corporation community, and the largely centralized control of the mass media of communications, and we see the dimensions of domination in American society; we see the measure of the impotence of the churches in face of the principalities and powers.

I share the conviction that Christian ethics must be promoted in direct confrontation with these principalities and powers. These principalities and powers have to be analyzed with the assistance of the behavioral sciences, which in turn are promoted by persons who, like us, are under the grip, even under the spell of the principalities and powers. From certain quarters we hear the term "the end of the ideologies." This term itself bespeaks an ideology. If we observe the confusion brought to a focus by the indictment of General Electric, Westinghouse, and other corporation executives; if we observe the extreme difficulty one encounters in the attempt to secure basic information regarding poverty in the United States; if we ask the question as to the contribution of the United Fruit Company to the rise of Castro; if we ask the question how the mass media are to be freed from their bondage to the process of marketing, we should be brought to an awareness of the epochal structural dimensions of our economy, and thus to an awareness of demands that the Lord of history places upon us at this time and in this place.

By Their Roots
Shall You Know Them

When Adams wrote, "By their roots shall you know them,"
he gave Jesus' familiar dictum, "By their fruits shall you know
them," a new twist. He accented the importance of histori-
cal roots in the nourishing of a strong personal and social
identity. Adams attributes the deep, continuing influence of
Jesus to his parables, original stories which make vivid and
available spiritual resources that otherwise would remain
hidden. The story of Jesus' life, the Gospel, is itself an ex-
tended parable of the life of radical faith. This address was
originally given at Meadville/Lombard Theological School
in 1984.—GKB

In the last line of Shelley's "A Defence of Poetry" we
read, "The poets are the unacknowledged legislators of
the world." We need to alter this axiom only slightly to
make it read, "Poetry is the unacknowledged legislator
of the world." You may recall that the principal rhetori-
cal devices of the poet are metaphor and simile. We
might say with Shelley that they are the great legislators guiding the mind toward or away from reality, ac-

tual or possible. Of course one can readily misfire or get mixed up in using metaphors. I recall that when I was teaching in a department of English in my first teaching job, I warned a student if, in his next theme he did not include an integrative metaphor, a clinching incident from history or fiction, he could expect his theme to be returned to him without grade. He turned in a theme on thrift, and the last line of the last paragraph was this sentence: "And so we see that a young man in his youth should save his money in order to have a nest egg to fall back on in his old age." I wrote on the margin at this point, "I hope that the egg will be a Chinese egg, in order to avoid a colorful splash."

We are all entirely familiar with the New Testament axiom, "By their fruits shall you know them," but since fruits cannot appear without roots, are we not entitled to say also, "By their roots shall you know them"? Hence, the root metaphor of this sermon will be "roots." In exploring our roots as liberals we may be able to achieve our sense of identity, thus answering in part the question, Who are we?

Since most of us Unitarian Universalists are "come-outers" from other denominations or from the streets (as is sometimes said) the task of identifying our roots is not an easy one. Indeed, as a historical denomination we must recognize many roots, for example, our roots in the left wing of the Reformation, in our congregational polity, in the Enlightenment and Romanticism, in the dialogue between religion and science in the nineteenth century. For the present discourse I, for the most part, will leave out of consideration these roots. I want to single out our rootage in the Bible and especially in the teachings of Jesus.

At the outset let us recall that one of the world-historical achievements of liberalism was higher criticism of the Bible by scholars, who during recent centuries have developed the methods of analyzing historical texts, tracing sources, or tracing even social-psychological motives for the selection and interpretation of texts. Accordingly, the idea of the absolute inerrancy of every word in Scripture has been widely abandoned. Indeed, some of this historical method has been so enlightening an enterprise that it has been taken up in part by leaders of other world religions.

One of the results of this whole endeavor was the distinction between the religion *of* Jesus and the religion *about* Jesus or between the religious outlook of Jesus himself and the christological doctrines that began to develop almost from the beginning. This distinction became ever clearer as the scholars recognized that much that is in the Gospels could not have come from Jesus. Hence, the texts employed by scholars to identify the religion *of* Jesus represent a much-reduced section of the Gospels. Regarding the religion *about* Jesus, the variety of interpretations available in the Scriptures is evident from the fact that in the New Testament one finds seventy-two different honorific titles given to him.

Now, in this whole matter, I want to refer to the work of a former eminent professor at Meadville, Dr. Clayton R. Bowen, the Frederick Henry Hedge Professor of New Testament Interpretation. I lament that I did not have the privilege of knowing him personally, for I arrived at Meadville two years after his death in 1934. In 1922 Dr. Bowen responded to a request from the American Unitarian Association to prepare a pamphlet. His pamphlet of eighteen pages (which was published in numerous editions) carries the title "Why are Unitarians Disciples of Jesus?" His answer to this question is that Unitarians are his disciples in that they adopt the religion *of* Jesus rather than a creedal statement *about* Jesus. Trinitarianism as a doctrine is not found in the New Testament.

Dr. Bowen speaks of Unitarians as "primitive believers, who go back, as no others do, to the original works of faith." He goes on to say, "I have never seen a creed I can imagine Jesus signing or saying. And somehow I can't hear him getting very far in a statement like the Apostles' Creed which asks him to say, 'I believe in God the Father almighty, maker of heaven and earth (yes, surely!) and in myself, his only Son. . . .' No, I think he would have to stop there." One encounters similar difficulties, Dr. Bowen says, if one reads these creedal formulas into the Beatitudes. "Blessed are the pure in heart, for they shall see the Father, the Son, and the Holy Ghost." "Blessed are the peacemakers, for they shall be called the children of the Blessed Trinity." "No," Dr. Bowen concludes, "This monstrous incongruity will not do. The Father is declared the only true God: that is the unitarianism of Jesus."

What is more important for our purpose is Dr. Bowen's description in his other writings on the religion of Jesus and especially of Jesus' conception of the kingdom or the reign of God. At the beginning of the present century Albert Schweitzer had thrown a bombshell into the whole discussion. Schweitzer, before he went to Africa, made a survey of the more important books of the nineteenth century on the kingdom of God. The bombshell thrown by Schweitzer held that absolutely everything in the Gospels is to be interpreted in the light of Jesus' expectation that the kingdom was to come very soon, bringing a new heaven and a new earth. The kingdom is only for the future, and its ethic only an interim ethic. This view of Schweitzer's had been discussed for over twenty years when Dr. Bowen with audacity published an essay to argue that for Jesus the eschatology was only of secondary interest, in short, that Jesus felt that the reign, the kingdom, of God, was not only to come in the future but was already breaking in, calling for the human response of change of heart, mind, and soul. Men and women, said Dr. Bowen, were to live as if the kingdom were already here. One need not wait for the Messiah. As an expression of this in-breaking power of the kingdom, Jesus went about healing the sick, also carrying the message of hope to the despised and neglected, to tax collectors, to prostitutes, to the downtrodden. Dr. Bowen rejected the merely futuristic view of Schweitzer.

What was Jesus' view of the working of the reign of God? Now we come to a mark of the genius of Jesus, the creator of the great parables, the employer of metaphor and simile. Dr. Bowen did not write extensively on the parables, but he wrote eloquently on Jesus the poet. Indeed, he adopted the idea that the utterances of Jesus in the parables are so expressive of a gifted person that they must be genuinely his and not the inventions of others.

Here, then, we see an independent young man who, faced with a great variety of vague and conflicting conceptions of the kingdom, of the Messiah, and of the Last Things, created parables of stunning simplicity which can be read with understanding by men and women of all times and places. The kingdom is like unto a seed that grows of itself, even when people are sleeping, it is like a tiny grain of mustard seed that people took and sowed in the fields, or it is like a pearl of great price sought by a merchant.

Several important things are to be observed here. No appeal is made to scriptural sanction or to supernatural revelation, and no fixed program is offered. Instead, Jesus uses a rational method of analogy appealing to empirical experience self-evident to Jew, gentile, or Samaritan. He selects processes in nature and lifts them up to illumine a gift, a reign that is at hand, available, mysterious, hidden and to become manifest, now in our midst, a creative power not of human making but offering new possibility. Instead of appealing to authorities Jesus says, "He that hath ears to hear, let him hear."

So what do we have here? We have the claim that there is a sovereign, universal moral law, a nonmanipulable reality, worthy alone of ultimate loyalty, and the source of peace and human fulfillment. This by the way is what the Unitarian philosophers Henry Nelson Wieman and Charles Hartshorne and Alfred North Whitehead have called their philosophy or theology of creativity.

In his sayings, stories, and actions Jesus not only gives religious-ethical application to the parables, he also discloses ample evidence of his roots in Hebrew piety (and even in Zoroastrian religion). He had his roots there, and thus he turns out himself to possess a cluster of roots. From these roots he derives his convictions that the seed that grows of itself sustains and supports and demands righteousness, a universal moral law informing the conscience and engendering just and merciful community. The response to the seed is the creative power of love. This love is not primarily an emotion, but rather energetic good will. In response to the growing seed all men and women are viewed as equal, indeed, even those who in human eyes appear to be unworthy. These are the fruits of the roots.

More than that, Jesus held that with him a new period in history was beginning following upon that of the law and the prophets, a period in which the ceremonial laws of Moses would be transcended and would find their essential meaning and purpose. Because of his special role in the new period, Dr. Bowen asserts, "the personality and word of Jesus together make up the Gospel."

Accordingly, the search for a christology, a conception of the theological significance of Jesus, is inevitable.

The new period would experience birth pangs, for all human institutions were to be challenged: the synagogue, the family, the cultural order. In this direction Jesus insisted that the sabbath was made for humans, not humans for the sabbath, and with small cords drove the money changers out of the Temple. This totalistic perspective regarding the culture appears in the imagery of St. Paul when he asserts that at the Last Day of Judgment Jesus Christ will approach the Father Almighty with all of the redeemed, including the redeemed institutions. The vision of Jesus, then, was not confined to a pietism or individualism that sees the meaning of life only in interpersonal relations.

I once heard the theologian-poet W. H. Auden answer a question about Shelley's dictum. He was asked, "Do you agree that the poets are the unacknowledged legislators of the world?" He pondered for a moment, and then in his typically gruff manner said, "The poet? Certainly not. Who are these legislators? I would say—the secret police." Auden's comment gives us occasion to say that the naturistic image of the seed that grows of itself is not the whole story, nature is also red in tooth and claw.

Jesus believed that a cosmic struggle between the divine and the demonic was underway, a struggle against greed, callousness, intolerance, and injustice. Here the ancient teachings of the Old Testament prophets are evident with a new urgency and a totalistic demand and promise.

For all of those who would accept this challenge Jesus is a vital root, though one of the most eminent of our liberal theologians of the twentieth century, Ernst Troeltsch, often said there may be other roots of this sort in the past or in the future.

The special quality of Jesus' teachings is, however, to be discerned in the parables. By devising these parables Jesus points beyond himself to the gift, the potential reign of the mysterious good that is beyond our comprehension. This mystery is a creative, sustaining, commanding, judging, community-forming and -transforming power that grows not old, ever calling for individual and corporate response.

Association
and Action

The question will ever be posed: What is the essence of liberalism? And so it is today. In order to answer this question we must, of course, have the courage not to over-simplify. A vital liberalism has within it tensions, struggle, a dialectic if you will. With a self-denying ordinance which disclaims finality or authoritativeness, we venture the following characterization of the essential elements of liberalism.

First, liberalism holds that nothing is complete, and thus nothing is exempt from criticism. Liberalism itself, as an actuality, is patient of this limitation. At best, even our symbols of communication are only referends and do not "capsule" reality. Stating this principle in religious terms, we may say that liberalism presupposes that revelation is continuous in word, in deed, and in nature, that it is not sealed, and that it points always beyond itself. Not only is significant novelty both possible and manifest, but also significance is itself inchoate and subject to inner tensions of peril and opportunity, of self-assertion and dependence.

Second, liberalism holds that all relations between persons ought ideally to rest on mutual free consent and not on coercion. Obviously, this principle cannot be advocated in any strict or absolute sense. It presupposes moral obligations; moreover, it is in fact operative in institutions which maintain continuity in one way or another with those of a previous epoch and order. Education, for example, may be compulsory within the liberal state, if not in the liberal church. All responsible liberals recognize the necessity for restrictions on individual freedom. Moreover, they recognize that "persuasion" can be perverted into a camouflage for duress. This second principle, like the others, can be stated in religious terms in various ways. For the sake of brevity we feature the statement familiar to religious liberals: All men and women are children of one God. The implication intended here is that the liberal method of free inquiry is the *conditio sine qua non* of both the fullest apprehension of the divine and the preservation of human dignity which comes from our being children of one God.

Third, being an ethical procedure, that is, purporting to be significant for human behavior, liberalism involves the moral obligation to direct one's efforts towards the establishment of democratic community. A full definition of the term "community" need not be attempted here. It involves, of course, a common life which gives rise to the expression of the manifold, creative impulses of the human spirit, an expression which presupposes a cooperative life impelled by the motives of love and justice. The statement of this principle in religious terms implies the other principles here adumbrate, and especially the fourth one. It will suffice to say here that the moral obligation which makes for community rests upon the divine imperative which demands mutuality, a condition of existence itself, as well as of love and justice. And it is also this which makes the role of the prophet central and indispensable in liberalism.

Fourth, liberalism holds that the resources (human divine) which are available for the achievement of meaningful change justify an attitude of ultimate optimism. This does not necessarily involve immediate optimism. In religious terms this principle may be stated thus: The divine element in reality both demands and supports mutuality. Thus the ground of hope is the prevenient and the actual grace of God.

We may now return to the previous question. Why liberal? And we answer: Because confidence in the principles of liberalism is the only effective resistant to ultimate skepticism and despair on the one side and to blasphemous claims to authority and suppressions of criticism on the other. These are the enemies of the human spirit whose dangers are threatening today.

—"Why Liberal?", James Luther Adams, 1939

Our Responsibility in Society

Adams develops several themes in this essay that are central to his thought: faith as "response to reliable power," the institutional consequences of religious beliefs, the free church tradition of "radical laicism" and its relation to the dispersion of power in a democracy, and the calling of all persons to engagement in political life—"the vocation of social responsibility." This essay was originally published in 1953.—GKB

I will pour out my Spirit on all flesh.
                                    —Joel 2:28, Acts 2:17

Our age is an "age of anxiety," a "time of troubles." None among us has escaped the anxiety, though the troubles have come nearer to some than to others. Well do I remember Dr. van Holk's address at the 1938 conference of the International Association for Religious Freedom at Bentveld, Holland, when he predicted that before another such conference would be held, a world war would probably intervene and that consequently some of us then present would not meet each other again.

The fulfillment of that prediction makes the heart heavy, not only because we lament the sufferings and

153

the casualties it has entailed but also because we know that these sufferings were the consequences of irresponsibility, and indeed partly of our irresponsibility. When we say "our irresponsibility," however, we have in mind not merely the unwise collective decisions of international politics but also what lay behind these decisions: our own personal irresponsibility.

For most of us, personal irresponsibility in these matters is not the result of indolence; it is the consequence of misguided energy and devotion. Of this misguided devotion we find a telling parable in Thomas Mann's novel *Dr. Faustus*. In Mann's hero, or perhaps we should call him the antihero, we may see on a wide canvas the projection of personal irresponsibility. Adrien Leverkuhn, Thomas Mann's Faustus, made a compact with the devil, agreeing that in return for fame as a composer he would sever bonds of normal affection and social responsibility. The outcome was disaster for Adrien and also for his nation: his disease became endemic.

This sort of compact with Satan, we know, has often been made, and not only by artists who claim to remain "above the battle." Some of us make the compact under the aegis of a pseudo-Protestant doctrine of vocation: we are prone to take seriously only the responsibility of doing our own professional or vocational work well. In this fashion we evade a costing responsibility for the social policies of the common life. One can find physicians, lawyers, professors, workers who believe that their public responsibilities consist almost entirely in their vocational activity. Many clergy believe that they can be better parish priests if they keep themselves aloof from the controversies of the marketplace and the civic forum. In a time when the slogan that the customer is always right widely prevails, many men and women renounce vigorous participation in community conflicts on the ground not only that they will otherwise jeopardize the high quality of their own work but also that they will offend their customers or clientele if they take a public stand in favor of unpopular causes. The profile of this sort of underling (to use Dostoyevski's term) appears in a tombstone epitaph that Dean Willard Sperry of Harvard Divinity School tells us he once saw in Scotland:

Here lies John McDonald
Born a man
Died a grocer.

The Hitlers of any age or community are always grateful for, indeed they rely on, the sins of omission committed by these retreating, uncreative eunuchs. As Thomas Mann's parable suggests, this compact for personal success is scarcely reliable. The compact protects the illusion that we are assuming responsibility when in fact we are only personally "getting ahead."

Response to Reliable Power

The Free Christian's sense of responsibility in society issues from concern for something more reliable than the desire for personal success. It issues from the experience of and the demand for community. For the Free Christian, responsibility is a response to the Deed that was "in the beginning," to the Deed of Agape that gave birth to the Christian community. It begins in the indicative mood and ends in the imperative. It is the response to that divine, self-giving, sacrificial love that creates and continually transforms a community of persons. This response by which community is formed and transformed is the process whereby men and women in obedience, freedom, and fellowship come to know God and to enjoy him. Responsibility is response to a divinely given community-forming power; the early Christians spoke of it as "living in Christ," as God's pouring forth of his spirit.

Irresponsibility is not a lack of response. Nor is it indifference or neutrality. It is a response to unreliable powers. Social irresponsibility is a response that expresses the obverse side of love; it is, in biblical language, the working of the Wrath of God. It issues in distress and distortion; and it injures the "just" as well as the "unjust," the responsible as well as the irresponsible.

In the historical community, in the fate of living together, women and men confront the divine powers that form community and the perverting powers that destroy it. They confront these powers not only in themselves and in individual persons but also in the forces that assume impersonal, institutional form. Indeed, the quality of individual personal existence is partly conditioned by the institutional patterns that constitute the body politic. Thus every personal problem is a social problem and every social problem is a personal problem.

Not that the human being is completely expressed or enclosed in the institutional forms. A person is not merely the precipitate of social-institutional forces, but a creature with roots in immemorial being. Or, to use a characteristically Protestant formulation, the person stands directly before God, ever subject to renewal that depends for its initiative upon some vitality beneath the actual, dated forms of institutional existence. But this extra–institutional dimension of persons is capable also of expressing a distortion of spirit; it is capable of expressing wrath as well as love.

For both the personal existence and the less personal, institutional existence, love is "the dearest freshness [of] deep down things," the dynamic ground of viable and meaningful community. It is the divine "call" to humanity, the divine initiative issuing a call to freedom and obedience and fellowship. The very meaning of history is to be found in the struggle for community, working toward the fulfillment of humanity and of the divine purpose. In this struggle the only reliable "object" of faith and devotion is Agape, the power of God which reconciles and reunites.

Love Made Concrete in the New Community

These words about love, the power of God, freedom and fellowship, are sufficiently familiar among us. But again and again we must ask, What do they mean? We must ask because one of the principal obstructions to the working of the power of God—one of the principal obstructions to response and responsibility—is an enervating devotion to mere abstractions. The adequate answer to the question must be a concrete answer. Responsibility is an incarnational response to the divine power of love, a response not only in personal but also in institutional behavior.

This demand of Agape for institutional expression is to be observed already in the early Christian community. Indeed, we see what the early Christians really meant by love, not only through observing their personal attitudes but also by looking at the kind of community which they believed to be demanded by love, and at the corresponding forms of responsibility involved.

For the most part the members of the primitive church were people who had previously been denied the dignity of responsibility in the shaping of policies of "church" and state. Membership in the Christian church released them from this low estate. To be sure, it would be false to assume that the early church aimed directly to bring about a revolution against this situation in politics; theirs was not in the usual sense a social revolution. Yet, they did insatiate a revolution. The response of these people to the power of God produced not only a new depth and intimacy in personal relations; it issued also in a new organization, in a church in which social responsibility and skill in administration were required.

This new community's influence in the creation of a sense of responsibility is evident from the very beginning; fishermen, artisans, women, and even slaves working together under the power of the Spirit became leaders or responsibly supported the missionary leaders and teachers. Moreover, the responsibilities assumed extended even beyond the strictly ecclesiastical functions. From the research of scholars we learn that the Christians of the first and second centuries formed charitable organizations and employment bureaus; they devised ways also for giving vocational education to orphans within the church. These practices, we must recognize, were an expression of the unfolding Christian conception of Agape, the concern under God for the good of the self, the other, and the community.

This assumption of responsibility on the part of ordinary people was of no small moment in the total context of antiquity. It acquired world-historical significance, for example, when the Roman Empire "fell." Indeed, these responsible ordinary people cushioned the "fall" and hastened the recovery. Scattered over the Mediterranean world there were hundreds of communities of people accustomed to performing special and skilled functions in social organizations. The recovery of the West from the Visigothic invasions would have required centuries longer than it did, had it not been for the sense of responsibility that had issued from the Christian response to the community-forming power of God. The Free Christianity of our modern devotion, as we shall presently show, owes its origin to essentially this same impulse.

The Institutional Consequences of Belief

A highly significant method for understanding the meaning of responsibility, and even of religious-ethical ideas in general, is illustrated by our account of early Christianity. Charles Peirce, the American logician and the teacher of William James, has proposed that an idea becomes clear only when we determine the habits of behavior that follow from it. We have seen that the meaning of the religious-ethical idea of Agape becomes clear only when we determine the habits, personal and institutional, that followed from it.

On the basis of this method of observation we may state a general principle: The meaning of "God" for human experience, and the meaning of response to the power of God, is to be determined in large part by observing the institutional consequences, the aspects of institutional life which the "believers" wish to retain or to change. Paul, Aquinas, Luther, Münzer, and Roger Williams all use the words *God, Spirit, love.* But these realities and concepts assume quite different meanings for these men, differences that can be discriminated in their various conceptions of the appropriate forms of state, church, family, school, and society, and in the corresponding interpretations of social responsibility.[1]

Christian history exhibits a variety of social and political outlooks that have claimed a Christian sanction. At different times Christians have demanded the rule of the free Spirit of God (pneumatocracy), theocracy, absolute monarchy, constitutional monarchy, sectarian communism, constitutional democracy, democratic religious socialism. Each of these views has been conditioned by profound changes in the climate of opinion and in historical circumstance. Each has claimed to be the will of God. The differences between the conceptions of God become evident in the differing conceptions of society and of social responsibility.

The Free Christian conception of the power of God becomes clear in certain of its major expressions if we recall that initially, in the sixteenth and seventeenth centuries, it entailed a new conception of Spirit and of the church and a new kind of social responsibility within and beyond that church. Indeed these new conceptions in part harked back to the outlook of the early church which we have been considering. Stressing the creative power of God for the formation of the free community, our spiritual ancestors centered attention on the day of Pentecost when the prophecy of Joel was, in their view, fulfilled: "I will pour out my Spirit on all flesh."

From the Joachites of the thirteenth century down through the Anabaptists, the Baptists, and the Dutch

Calvinists of the sixteenth century, to the English Independents and other aggressive sects of the seventeenth century, we can trace the development of a group of doctrines and practices that were destined to alter the shape of Protestantism and of modern society: a new spirit of toleration, a revived conception of the Holy Spirit and of the earlier doctrine of the church. Some of these sects were imbued with the Calvinist conception of the sovereignty of God with its demand for the establishment of the holy community. Some of them interpreted the meaning of history in terms of the struggle between different conceptions of church and community; they viewed the major phases of church history as the epochs or dispensations of the struggle between God and Satan. (The very title of the book *The Fall of Christianity,* by the Dutch theologian G. J. Heering, is reminiscent of this view, according to which the loss of the early type of church organization was itself the fall of the church.) These early sects of the modern period, in calling for a return to the primitive church organization, also aimed to be the heralds of a new age; Joachim of Fiore called it the Third Era, the era of the Spirit which would bring with it the Church of the Spirit.[2] In our day this movement, with its subsequent issue, is called the Radical Reformation.

This left wing movement wrought a great social revolution in whose heritage we are still living, a revolution analogous to that wrought by the early Christians. The latter-day revolution was carried out in opposition not only to Roman Catholicism but also to the right wing of the Reformation—orthodox Lutheranism and Calvinism. Authority in the right wing of the Reformation and in Roman Catholicism remained in many essentials the same. The doctrine of justification by faith in Lutheranism and of the sovereignty of God in orthodox Calvinism did not in essence do away with the authoritarian structure of the church. Some writers today even assert that there are analogies between the authoritarianism of Calvinist theocracy and that of Russian communism; we are familiar also with the view that the authoritarian structures of Roman Catholicism and of Russian communism bear analogies (which, to be sure, can be overstated). In this struggle between the left and the right wings we can discern the principal motif of modern history.

Radical Laicism and the Dispersion of Power

We of the Free Church tradition should never forget, or permit our contemporaries to forget, that the decisive resistance to authoritarianism in both church and state, and the beginning of modern democracy, appeared first in the church and not in the political order. The churches of the left wing of the Reformation held that the churches of the right wing had effected only half a reformation. They gave to Pentecost a new and extended meaning. They demanded a church in which every member, under the power of the Spirit, would have the privilege and the responsibility of interpreting the Gospel and also of assisting to determine the policy of the church. The new church was to make way for a radical laicism—that is, for the priesthood and the prophethood of all believers. "The Spirit blows where it lists."

Out of this rediscovery of the doctrine of the Spirit came the principles of Independency: local autonomy, free discussion, the rejection of coercion and of the ideal of uniformity, the protection of minorities, the separation of church and state. Power and responsibility were to be dispersed. In a fashion not unlike that of the primitive church, the doctrine of the Spirit became the sanction for a new kind of social organization and of social responsibility. A new church was born, and with it a new age.

Once released, the new spirit poured forth into all areas of society. It could not be kept within the bounds of church life. First, it was carried over into the sphere of the state. The Independents began to say, "If we are responsible to God for the kind of church we have, we are responsible also for the kind of state we have. If it is wrong to be coerced by church authorities, it is wrong to be dominated by political authorities. As children of God, we ought to have a greater share of power and responsibility in the state as well as in the church." By analogy the conception of a new church in a new age was extended to include the demand for a democratic state and society. Thus the democratic state is in part the descendant of the Church of the Spirit.

These principles were not enunciated without dust and heat. Nor did they spring into existence suddenly.

They were promoted by certain branches of the left wing in various countries and with differing emphases. Not all of the churches, for example, demanded the separation of church and state.

The movement in Britain has been characterized by no one better than by the Roman Catholic historian Lord Acton. Let me quote his words.

For it is by the sects, including the Independents, that the English added to what was done by Luther and Calvin, and advanced beyond the sixteenth-century ideas.

The power of Independency was not in relation to theology, but to Church government. They did not admit the finality of doctrinal formulas, but awaited the development of truth to come. Each congregation governed itself independently, and every member of the church participated in its administration. There was consocation, but not subordination. The Church was governed, not by the State or by bishops or by the presbytery, but by the multitude of which it was composed. It was the ideal of local selfgovernment and of democracy. . . .

The political consequences reached far. The supremacy of the people, being accepted in Church government, could not be repudiated in the State. There was a strong prejudice in its favour. "We are not over one another," said Robinson, "but one with another." They inclined not only to liberty, but equality, and rejected the authority of the past and the control of the living by the dead. . . . Persecution was declared to be spiritual murder. All sects alike were to be free, and Catholics, Jews, and Turks as well.[3]

Out of this soil of early Free Church doctrine and experience emerged also the principles of connectionalism and federalism, principles that represent attempts to come to terms with the social necessity of achieving integration as well as with the demand for a dispersion of power and responsibility.

In church, state, and society, then, the aggressive sects provided the institutional patterns for the assumption of initiative and responsibility on the part of all members. Political as well as ecclesiastical authorities were asserted to be responsible to the people, and all were responsible to God. In contrast to the right wing principles of domination and hierarchy, the institutional principles of persuasion and coarchy became the signature of the epoch of the Free Church. The watchword of this new epoch was uttered succinctly by a certain Colonel Rainsborough who in the Army Debates of the Cromwellian period said, "Every English he hath his own contribution to make."

In the course of time the new doctrine of the church was applied also beyond the areas of ecclesiastical and political organization. It worked to dissolve the patterns of domination in family and school as well. In all of these areas the existing authorities were made responsible or responsive to other members of the organization. Eventually the patriarchal family authority began to yield to a more democratic authority—to what we today call a permissive atmosphere. The schoolmaster came to recognize the intrinsic dignity of the pupil.

The Free Churches and the Growth of Democracy

But the influence of this new conception of the church and of the responsibility of each person reached even beyond the institutions of church, state, school, and family. This influence is to be observed especially in the emergence of an institution that some historians and political scientists consider to be the characteristic and decisive instrument of the democratic society, namely, the voluntary association. The voluntary organization provides the opportunity for ever wider and wider dispersion of responsibility, for the displacement of hierarchy (though it can never rightly dispense with hierarchy altogether, for that way lies chaos). It stands between the individual and the state, and also between the church and the state; and it is controlled by neither the state nor the church. An essential pattern of the voluntary organization was already present in the church of the voluntary covenant and also in the voluntary business association. The many committees and organizations that exist in the modern community, the organizations that work for social reform, for cooperative production or distribution of goods, for the protection of civil rights, for the protection or extension of suffrage, for the maintenance of professional standards, for the promotion of new legislation, and for a thousand and one other purposes that are pursued by the free citizen in a modern democracy, represent the application of the original Free Church idea to organized efforts that serve to shape the policy of the modern community in politics and in commerce, in social welfare and in leisure-time activity. All of these forms of association, including the modern trade union, are in large part the outgrowth of left wing Protestantism; indeed, they may be characterized as the secularization of the Free Church doctrine of the church.[4] Because of just this process of the secularization of the religious groups, Adolph Lowe, the German sociologist, is able to summarize the British experience in the following way:

> It would be a misinterpretation of the facts if we were to equate English liberalism with an atomistic structure of society. What strikes the observer of this period of English history who compares England with the great continental nations, is not an extreme individualism, but the general tendency to form voluntary associations. From the political parties down to the chapel meetings, public life was actually dominated by self-governing bodies, growing up spontaneously but submitting to the principle of democratic leadership.[5]

The mitigation of hierarchy in favor of coarchy and democratic leadership is to be seen today in one of the major innovations in business enterprise. Increasingly, the modern business executive recognizes that high productivity depends on morale, and that high morale depends on the dispersion of responsibility and initiative. Associated with this tendency is the recent development of group dynamics, the effort to delineate the principles whereby universal participation may be elicited and whereby group morale and "productivity" in group consensus may be increased. These efforts presuppose that the abiding strength and spiritual validity of any group depend on a diversity of interests united by more general purposes, that they depend on the power of every member and group to get a hearing. They offer a dramatic illustration of the axiom enunciated by Colonel Rainsborough and of the conception of human being also expressed by Goethe in his couplet:

Had Allah meant me for a worm
In shape of a worm he had formed me.

I have mentioned mainly the English Nonconformists. Obviously, other Protestant churches have contributed to the growth of the conception of social responsibility made explicit in the English Free Church tradition. One could trace a similar lineage of development in the United States' experience. The U.S. Constitution and the Federalist Papers are not understandable apart from the historical background of Free Church doctrine and Free Church pluralism. And as for federalism, where could one better study its provenance than in Swiss Protestantism? One could cite a similarly rich heritage in the Netherlands, showing the ways "spiritualist" doctrines and the conception of religious freedom have exercised their influence.

It is precisely in those countries where the left wing doctrines have not become decisive that one finds even today a persistence of the traditions of domination and obedience. The Soviet Union, Germany, and Italy have grievously suffered from tyranny as a partial consequence of the fact that Free Church conceptions of responsibility and of the dispersion of power were held in check. In these countries democratic tendencies in the national life have been relatively weaker than in the countries of a continuing left wing protestantism for the countries of the right wing tend to favor conformity rather than discussion.[6]

The eminent German jurist Otto von Gierke has suggested that the major struggle in Western history since the time of Charlemagne has been the struggle between the rival conceptions of community which we have characterized as those of the right wing and the left wing. On the one side we have what von Gierke calls "the lordly union," the society or group in which authority emanates from the top down; against this, we have the society or group that aims to have authority emanate from the bottom of the social pyramid, from the consensus of the "grass roots." In both types of community we find that conceptions of God, love, human being, are appealed to; but these conceptions take on radically different meanings in terms of the different types of consensus favored. The consensus that appears in "the lordly union" tends to be one imposed by a vicar of God or an equivalent authority; the "grass roots" consensus aims to recognize that the Holy Spirit blows where it lists and that people are more likely to yield to that Spirit when they do not blasphemously intrude their own human chain of command.

The Vocation of Social Responsibility

Now, within this brief and elliptical survey of the left wing of the Reformation, which has exercised its influence in all of the churches represented in our International Association for Religious Freedom, we find the context for the understanding of our responsibility in society. Our responsibility is to maintain the heritage that is ours, the heritage of response to the community-forming Power that we confront in the Gospels and in the Free Churches. This community-forming Power calls us to the affirmation of that abundant love which is not ultimately in our possession but is a holy gift. It is the ground and goal of our vocation.

But this vocation cannot be carried out if we try merely to repeat the behavior of our ancestors. In important respects our historical situation is unique. The struggle between the left wing and the right wing is taking new forms. We live in a time when both the theology and the social principles of the old liberalism are under attack.

Today we confront the neo-Reformation movement in Protestant theology. From this source some of us may find certain theological correctives with respect to the ultimate issues of life as liberals have interpreted them. But this neo-Reformation movement in some circles carries with it such a nostalgia for the "pure doctrine" of the past that it also revives the doctrine of the authoritarian church. An authoritarian church is a danger to the free society as well as to the free church. This fact should make us scrutinize the more carefully the "pure doctrine" that is offered. It should make us aware of the present-day need for a neo-Radical Reformation which will creatively resist the patterns of domination and of rigidly conformist obedience.

In our day we confront also the impersonal forces of a mass society with its technological devices for producing stereotyped opinion. In this mass society the individual is always in danger of becoming lost in the "lonely crowd." One is attacked by a stream of prepared "ideas" and "facts" that issue from the endless transmission belts of radio, movie, and press. These "opinion industries" provide a poor substitute for a community of faith. Insofar as they form community at all, it is for the most part the "community" of support for special interests—the interests of nationalism, racism, and business as usual. In large measure this "community" is an instrument manipulated and exploited by central power groups. In short, it is a form of authoritarianism. It is the modern, anonymous version of the earlier imposed direction from the top in face of which the primitive Christian church and the left wing of the Reformation protested in the name of a more intimate, personal community dependent on individual dignity and responsibility.

But there are even more destructive forces that threaten freedom of the spirit. The great economic dislocations of our time have given the age a neurotic character. These dislocations cannot be corrected by our merely exhorting ourselves and others to individual initiative and responsibility; they require concerted analysis and attack. It may be that these dislocations and the exigencies of international conflict will require even more centralized controls than we are now accustomed to. Thus the growth of the patterns of authority characteristic of the traditional mass church may be an unavoidable fate for our time. All the more, then, is our heritage of the left wing threatened and needed. At the same time we face the danger that the small-group organization will become merely a sanction for large-group irresponsibilities.

The revived neo-orthodoxy, the new mass society manipulated by pressure groups, the increase of planning, the fear of the totalitarianism in the East, taken together with modern vocational specialization, have

conspired against our maintaining our heritage in a vital way within even our own churches; and they also
have made the more difficult the meeting of our social
responsibilities through participation in the policy-shap-
ing activities of the community.

It is just here, then, that we encounter our peculiar
responsibility in society, the responsibility to offer a
church in which there is an explicit faith in the community-forming power of God, a practice of the disciplines of liberty, an eliciting of the participation of our
own membership in creative fellowship. From such a
fellowship, concerned to extend the community in
which all persons may be encouraged to make their own
contribution, our members can meet their social responsibilities by expressing in the other areas of life—in the
state, the family, the school, the voluntary association,
and industry—the response to the love that will not let
us go. This movement of the patterns of responsibility
from the church to these other areas of life, as we have
seen, has taken place since the very beginning of our
Free Christianity. It is our social responsibility to maintain and extend this movement in face of human needs
for health and shelter and for a world in which (across
the lines of race and class and nation) all may enjoy their
God-given dignity and responsibility—for a world in
which Everyone can make a contribution. If we do not
participate in groups that work deliberately for these
ends, we are ourselves irresponsible; we are dominated
underlings—mass people in compact with Satan.

Here, then, is the vocation placed upon us by the promise of old, "I will pour out my Spirit on all flesh." For us who bear the heritage of Free Christianity, the promise draws and binds us together. The promise is ultimately not one that we make to ourselves. It is one that we receive in faith. Yet it is also a promise whose fulfillment is contingent upon our response in responsibility.

In our time of troubles the problems are vast in their dimensions. But they were vast also in the birth period of the primitive church and in the birth period of our Free Churches. To cringe in despair of ourselves is to despair of the divine promise. It is to forget that responsibility is response to a Spirit that is *given* to us—to the light that has shone and that still shines in the darkness.

Notes

1. It is questionable whether the method of "motif-research" promoted by the Swedish theologian Anders Nygren (*Agape and Eros*) is adequate. Nygren's method restricts itself to examining verbal doctrinal statements. But such a method overlooks very important and relevant facts. We may not assume that Paul and Luther, for example, employ the term *Agape* with the same meaning simply because they use the same theological terms to describe it. Their conceptions of church and state—in short, their conceptions of social responsibil-

ity—must be taken seriously into account if we are to grasp the distinctive elements in their conceptions of Christian love.

2. Unitarians in the U.S. are familiar with this phrase particularly through F. G. Peabody's book of a generation ago, *The Church of the Spirit*. European Christians have been reminded of it by Ernst Benz's remarkable study, *Ecclesia Spiritualis*.

3. John Emerich Edward Dalberg-Acton, *Lectures on Modern History* (London: Macmillan and Co., 1906) p. 200.

4. To be sure, many of these voluntary organizations have appeared within the shadow of the right wing, e.g., of Roman Catholicism, but the Church has sought always to keep them under ecclesiastical control. But not only the authoritarian Church has obstructed the free development of voluntary organization. Political dictatorships have always recognized the voluntary organization to be one of their principal enemies, for it provides the citizen with the opportunity of disseminating "dangerous thoughts" and of promoting social policies inimical to the power of the central authorities. Thomas Hobbes, the St. Simonians, the ultramontane Catholics, Hitler, and Mussolini, all agree that free-floating voluntary associations must be forbidden.

5. Adolph Lowe, *Economics and Sociology* (London: George Allen and Unwin, 1935).

6. One of the hopeful signs for democracy in Germany today appears in the marked advance shown by the "free-religious communities." Representatives of

these groups attended the Oxford Congress of the International Association for Religious Freedom. Especially impressive are the Evangelical Academies in Germany, the Netherlands, and Sweden as innovations in the direction of radical laicism.

The Indispensable Discipline
of Social Responsibility:
Voluntary Associations

Central among our freedoms, Adams affirms, is freedom of association. Because totalitarianisms of the left and the right target this basic freedom, engagement in voluntary associations is "the indispensable discipline of social responsibility." Adams asserts, "The voluntary association at its best offers an institutional framework within which the give and take of discussion may be brought under criticism and subjected to change. . . . In short, the voluntary association is a means for the institutionalizing of gradual revolution." Adams presented this address at the University of Padua, Italy, in 1962, following the Second Vatican Council, where he was a Protestant observer.—GKB

In 1927 in the city of Nuremberg, six years before the National Socialists came into power, I was watching a Sunday parade on the occasion of the annual mass rally of the Nazis. Thousands of youth, as a sign of their vigor and patriotism, had walked from various parts of Germany to attend the mass meeting of the party. As I watched the parade, which lasted for four hours and which was punctuated by trumpet and drum corps made up of hundreds of Nazis, I asked some people on the sidelines to explain to me the meaning of the swastika, which decorated many of the banners. Before very long I found myself engaged in a heated argument. Suddenly someone seized me from behind and pulled me by the elbows out of the group with which I was arguing. In the firm grip of someone whom I could barely see I was forced through the crowd and propelled down a side street and up into a dead-end alley. As this happened I assure you my palpitation rose quite perceptibly. I was beginning to feel Nazism existentially. At the end of the alley my uninvited host swung me around quickly, and he shouted at me in German, "You fool. Don't you know? In Germany today when you are watching a parade, you either keep your mouth shut, or you get your head bashed in." I thought he was going to bash it in right there. But then his face changed into a friendly smile and he said, "If you had continued that argument for five minutes longer, those fellows would have beaten you up." "Why did you decide to help me?" I asked. He replied, "I am an anti-Nazi. As I saw you there, getting into trouble, I thought of the times when in New York City as a sailor of the German merchant marine I received a wonderful hospitality. And I said to myself, 'Here is your chance to repay that hospitality.' So I grabbed you, and here we are. I am inviting you home to Sunday dinner."

This man turned out to be an unemployed worker. His home was a tenement apartment in the slums. To reach it, we climbed three flights up a staircase that was falling apart, and he ushered me into a barren room where his wife and three small children greeted their unexpected American guest in astonishment. We had the Sunday meal together, a dinner of greasy dumplings and of small beer drunk from a common jug. Within a period of two hours I learned vividly of the economic distress out of which Nazism was born. From this trade-union worker I learned also that one organization after the other that refused to bow to the Nazis was being threatened with compulsion. The totalitarian process had begun. Freedom of association was being abolished. "You keep your mouth shut, and you conform, or you get your head bashed in." A decade later in Germany I was to see at first hand the belated resistance of the churches to this attack upon freedom of speech and freedom of association.

At this juncture I had to confront a rather embarrassing question. I had to ask myself, What in your typical behavior as an American citizen have you done that would help to prevent the rise of authoritarian government in your own country? What disciplines of democracy (except voting) have you habitually undertaken with other people which could serve in any way directly to affect public policy? More bluntly stated: I asked myself, What precisely is the difference between you and a political idiot?

Freedom of Association

Immediately after the Second World War the Swiss theologian Karl Barth made a speaking tour in Germany, and in his talks he stressed the idea that every conscientious German citizen should now participate actively in voluntary associations committed to the task of making democracy work. I do not know whether Karl Barth as a professor in Germany practiced his own preaching when Nazism was on the rise. But in giving his admonition to the Germans after the war, he pointed to a characteristic feature of any democratic society, namely, freedom of association.

Every totalitarian theory rejects just this freedom. Indeed, the rejection of freedom of association, the rejection of the freedom to form groups that attempt democratically to affect public policy, can serve as the beginning of a definition of totalitarianism. We are familiar with the fulminations against freedom of association by Hobbes and Rousseau. Hobbes the totalitarian warns against "the great number of corporations which are as it were many lesser commonwealths in the body of a greater, like worms in the entrails of a natural man." The late Senator Joseph McCarthy worked in the spirit of Hobbes when he tried to smother freedom of association.

As against Hobbes the theorists of democracy have asserted that only through the exercise of freedom of association can consent of the governed become effective; only through the exercise of freedom of association can the citizen in a democracy participate in the process that gives shape to public opinion and to public policy. For this reason we may speak of the voluntary association as a distinctive and indispensable institution of democratic society.

How shall we define voluntary association? Speaking of the situation in the United States of over a hundred years ago, the Frenchman Alexis de Tocqueville observed that "in no country in the world has the principle of association been more successfully used, or applied to a greater multitude of objects, than in America. . . . Wherever, at the head of some new undertaking, you see the government in France, or a man of rank in England, in the United States you will be sure to find an association." De Tocqueville gives the classical description of the multitude of associations in the United States at that time, associations for libraries, hospitals, fire prevention, and for political and philanthropic purposes. One could sum up de Tocqueville's description of the United States at that time by saying that where two or three Americans are gathered together you may be sure that a committee is being formed. We have been "a nation of joiners."

Any healthy democratic society is a multigroup society. One finds in it business corporations, religious associations, trade unions, educational associations, recreational, philanthropic, protective, and political associations, and innumerable social clubs. These associations are, or claim to be, voluntary; they presuppose freedom on the part of the individual to be or not to be a member, to join or withdraw, or to consort with others to form a new association. By way of contrast the state and the family, for example, are as associations involuntary, and in some countries the church also is virtually involuntary. All persons willy-nilly are born into a particular state and a particular family. It is not a matter of choice whether they will belong to these two associations. In this sense they are involuntary. There are other associations, to be sure, that are difficult to classify under either category, voluntary or involuntary. Taken together, these associations, involuntary and voluntary, represent the institutional articulation of the pluralistic society.

The Historical Roots of Voluntary Associations

The appearance of the voluntary association in Western society did not come without struggle. The initial demand for voluntary association came from the churches of the Radical Reformation, especially the aggressive sects of the left wing Puritanism. These churches insisted that religion, in order to be a matter of choice, must be free from state control. Therefore they demanded the separation of church and state. This struggle for freedom of religious association continued for over two centuries. It was accompanied or followed by a struggle for freedom of economic association, for freedom to establish political parties, for freedom of workers to form unions, and for freedom to institute reforms in society. Not all voluntary associations, to be sure, are concerned with public policy. Some associations are simply social clubs, others promote hobbies, and still others are merely status groups. Considering the voluntary association that is concerned with social policy, for example with securing civil liberties or better housing, or with overcoming racial discrimination, we may say that this sort of association stands between the individual and the state and provides the instrumentality for achieving consensus within a group, and for implementing this consensus through either political or nonpolitical means. This sort of association provides the opportunity for discussion, for assembling neglected facts, and for scrutinizing and overcoming mere propaganda.

The voluntary association at its best offers an institutional framework within which the give and take of discussion may be promoted, an institutional framework within which a given consensus or practice may be brought under criticism and be subjected to change. It offers a means for bringing a variety of perspectives into interplay. It offers the means of breaking through old social structures in order to meet new needs. It is a means of dispersing power, in the sense that power is the capacity to participate in making social decisions. It is the training ground of the skills that are required for viable social existence in a democracy. In short, the voluntary association is a means for the institutionalizing of gradual revolution. The process often takes place through the entry into political history of groups hitherto hidden, silent, or suppressed. Here we think of the emergence of the middle class, of the professions, the blacks, and women—and today we see it on a continental scale in the "basic communities" of Latin America.

I have spoken of the fact that freedom of association was fought for by the churches of the left wing of the Reformation. Any adequate treatment of free association demands theological interpretation. Such a treatment would show how the doctrine of the covenant in old and New England was employed to sanction the priesthood and the prophethood of all believers, and thus to express religious and social responsibility. By covenant people responded to God's community-forming power. But the prime example of the institutionalization of a doctrine of the covenant is to be found much earlier in Western history. The primitive Christian church illustrates many of the features of a voluntary association which I have mentioned. In one sense, to be sure, the primitive church was not a voluntary association as ordinarily conceived. It was believed to have come into existence through the work of God and not through the acts of persons. Nor was it directly concerned with public policy as such, except that by its very existence it bespoke the demand for freedom of association. Yet the primitive church illustrates the dispersion of power and responsibility, and it illustrates also the breaking through of old social structures toward the end of creating new structures. The primitive church broke through the bonds of the ethnic religion of Judaism: Jew, Greek, Roman, and German could be members. Moreover, the membership of the primitive church came from all classes of society, but especially from the lower classes (including slaves). The church also gave a new status to women. Besides all this, the primitive church gave the common people the opportunity to learn the skills required for effective social organization. The common people who were members had to learn the skills of preaching and teaching, of administration, of missionizing, and also of dispersing charity. The emergence of the primitive church represents, then, one of the great innovative movements of history, a great social revolution. Probably the recovery of the West after the fall of Rome took place with greater speed because of the thousands of people who had been trained in skills that could be employed outside as well as inside the church organization. Here was an enormous dispersion of the capacity to participate in the making of social decision, and in response to a transcendent purpose.

By the time the church had come into its medieval form, however, a great change had taken place in its internal structure. Indeed, certain branches of the Reformation represented a protest against the monolithic power structure of the church, and they carried through this protest by appeal to the model of the primitive church. So we see movement back and forth from one kind of social structure to another.

Thus an association originally intended to disperse power and responsibility undergoes changes moving in the opposite direction, that is, in the direction of concentration of power. In the earliest essay in America on the structure of voluntary associations, William Ellery Channing, the Boston Unitarian clergyman, pointed to this danger. The voluntary association, so far from serving as an instrument of freedom, may end in becoming a new instrument of tyranny and conformism. Channing could speak with experience in these matters, for a number of the great reformist associations of the nineteenth century were organized in his study.

"The Iron Law of Oligarchy"

Robert Michels, the Italian sociologist, has given a memorable account of the internal shift of power that can take place in an association. His view is that in any organization the "eager beavers" can take advantage of the indolence of the average member. By this means they gain control of the organization. This process he describes as the operation of "the iron law of oligarchy."

We can observe the iron law of oligarchy as it operates in the great pressure groups of today. A few years ago some sociologists studied the centralized bureaucracy of the American Medical Association. They found a goodly number of physicians who said they felt that the A.M.A. through its policies was damaging the image of the physician in the United States today. On being asked why they did not do something to change the structure and the policies of the bureaucracy, some of them gave the answer, "I trained to be a doctor, and I want to practice medicine. In order to break the bureaucracy of the A.M.A., I and many of my colleagues would have to spend much more time than we can afford." It is a striking fact that the large business corporation functions by reducing the role of the shareholder. The average small shareholder surrenders power by signing a proxy to the representative of the managers. This sort of phenomenon belongs to the pathology of associations, and we could find ample illustration of it by examining colleges and churches.

But the pathology does not end with the functioning of the iron law of oligarchy within associations. It can be observed also in the functioning of the great pressure groups as they affect public policy. Legislation regarding the pressure groups has corrected some of the evils. But the role of the special interest pressure group today presents us with a major problem of the democratic society: The power of the pressure group is exercised through collusion with other pressure groups. The lobbyist of the wool growers' association in face of some legislation he wishes to impede goes to the representative of the copper producers' association and says, "I know that you are not interested pro or con in this bit of legislation, but if you will join us now, we shall give you assistance when you need it in a similar situation." In a society where the principle of freedom of association obtains, one to be sure must recognize the legitimate freedom of the pressure groups. Besides this, we must recognize they do not always enter into collusion. In some measure the great special interest pressure groups function as countervailing powers that neutralize each other. This neutralization, however, does not appear when, for example, the issue has to do with the distribution of the tax burden. Here the ordinary citizen gets shortchanged.

Two Types of Associations

This whole situation points to a major requirement for a viable and authentic democratic society. One can roughly classify the great voluntary associations concerned with public policy. The one type of association is called the special interest group. Here the association is judged by its capacity to ring up money on the cash register of the member. These special interest groups became very influential already at the end of the nineteenth century in the U.S.A. Henry Demarest Lloyd points out this changing character of American society. Speaking of the great concentrations of business power and of the large special interest pressure groups at the end of the century he said that the letters "U.S.A." had come to mean the "United Syndicates of America."

The other type of association is the sort that directly aims to promote the general welfare. The member of the association does not expect to make personal gain through the association. For example, the average member of the American Civil Liberties Union seldom makes a personal gain from participation in the organization. Members spend their time and money to support the effort to redefine the nature of civil liberties in a changing society, and also to defend those whose liberties are violated or threatened.

In some of the larger associations or pressure groups the broad constituency of the membership makes it possible for us to say that the gain of the members is a gain also for many nonmembers. For example, the civil rights movement with its many associations that aim to promote the liberty of the blacks will in the long run increase the productivity of the entire nation and it will also extend the rights of other underprivileged groups. The award of the Nobel Prize for peace to Martin Luther King Jr. served to recognize the contribution of civil rights organizations to the whole democratic society and even to the forces of emancipation in the world at large.

In face of these two types of association we can say that the health of democracy depends on the capacity of general welfare associations to function as countervailing powers against the narrower purposes of the special interest associations.

Now, I would like to make three brief observations with regard to this demand. First, let me mention the findings of some recent studies of college graduates. These studies indicate that insofar as they are concerned with public policy, most college graduates in the United

States are affiliated with special interest groups. Moreover, they give little attention or time to participation in the organizations; they simply pay their dues and expect the bureaucracy to look after their interests. Now, a second observation. A minister in Denver has published an elaborate study of the associational behavior of the members of his middle-class church. He shows that even the associations of philanthropic character to which his church members belong serve mainly to bring together birds of a feather, that is, to bring together people possessing the same economic and political prejudices. So far from extending the range of the community across ethnic and class lines, these associations serve to keep the classes and races separate. A third observation: Mirra Komarovsky has studied the associational behavior of the residents of Manhattan. She has found that apart from membership in the church the citizens of Manhattan do not on the average belong to even one association concerned with public policy. She asserts that we have here a good definition of the mass person. Regardless of whether one is "educated" or not, one is a mass person who does not participate in associations concerned with the public benefit. Being only on the receiving end of the mass media of communications, in the world of public policy such a person is a political eunuch.

Human sinfulness expresses itself, then, in the indifference of the average citizen who is impotent, so idiotic in the sense of that word's Greek root (that is, privatized), as not to exercise freedom of association for the sake of the general welfare and for the sake of becoming a responsible self.

Ernst Troeltsch has made a distinction that is of prime significance here. He distinguishes between what he calls subjective and objective virtues. Subjective virtues are virtues that can be exhibited in immediate person-to-person relations. Objective virtues require an institution for their expression. Thus, from the larger human perspective we can say that the isolated good man or woman is a chimera. There is no such thing as a "good person" as such. There is only the good father or the good mother, the good physician or the good plumber, the good churchperson, the good citizen. The good person of the subjective virtues, to be sure, provides the personal integrity of the individual; without it the viable society is not possible. But from the point of view of the *institutional* commonwealth the merely good individual is good for nothing. Moreover, the narrow range of responsibility of the man or woman who confines attention merely to family and job serves to dehumanize the self.

At the outset I spoke of the experience in pre-Nazi Germany when a man told me, "You either keep your mouth shut, or you get your head bashed in." In the democratic society the nonparticipating citizens bash their own heads in. The living democratic society requires the disciplines of discussion and common action for the determination of policy. The differences between persons are determined by the quality and direction of their participation. In this sense we may understand the New Testament word, "By their fruits shall you know them"; but to this word we should add the admonition, by their groups shall you know them.

Theological Bases
of Social Action

Among Adams's essays, this is one of the most intellectually demanding. He draws on Plato, Max Weber, and Ernst Troeltsch. He also quotes Emerson: "All power is of one kind, a sharing in the nature of the world." As an ethicist Adams put more stock in consequences than in conscience; thus he was more concerned with social ethics and justice than with personal ethics and virtue. In this perspective a central concept of social ethics is power, the capacity to influence and, as Adams here accents, "the capacity to be influenced." God is not "raw power" (power over), in his view, but enabling power (power with). Power, then, is the foundational concept in the analysis. This essay was originally published in two parts, in 1950 and 1951.—GKB

The decisive element in social action is the exercise of power, and the character of social action is determined by the character of the power expressed. Power has always a double character: first, as the expression of God's law and love; second, as the exercise of human freedom. To understand power as God's law and love is to under-

195

stand it as Being; to understand it as human freedom is to understand it as the person's response to the possibilities of being, a response which is both individual and institutional. All response is therefore social action in the broad sense and also in the narrower sense of group action for the achievement of consensus with respect to the shaping of social policy. Both of these types of social action are expressions of necessity as well as of freedom. The expression of power in the dimensions of both freedom and necessity must be understood by the Christian in terms of its theological bases. The definition of the theological bases of social action must be achieved in terms of the ultimate purposes and resources of human life; it must be achieved equally in terms of the threats to the fulfillment of these purposes. Taken together, God's law and human freedom operate for the creation of community or, through God's wrath, for its destruction. According to the Judeo-Christian view of God's law and love, it is the destiny of men and women to love and to be loved; there is an interdependence of spiritual destinies; this is the "plan of salvation." All response on the part of men and women to God's law and love is social action in the broad sense, whether the response furthers community or perverts and destroys it.

Much social thought has misunderstood or ignored the dual character of power as divine law and human response. The misunderstanding has come out of exclusive preoccupation with the dimension of human freedom and the ignoring of the dimension of divine law. It is not enough to say with Henry Adams that "power is poison" or with Jacob Burckhardt that "power is by its nature evil, whoever wields it." The power that is law understood as God's is not in itself evil; it is the ground for the possibility of exercising power for good or evil. Acton's assertion that "power tends to corrupt, and absolute power corrupts absolutely" is true as he understood it, namely, as applying only to human freedom, the social-political dimension. Power can be understood to corrupt absolutely only when the social-political power is sundered from its theological ground, God's law and love. This was Acton's understanding of the meaning of his famous aphorism. Contemporary social thought has tended to lift the dictum out of its total context. When accepted so superficially, such dicta give plausibility to Candide's admonition that in a world of corruption we should simply cultivate our own garden. This interpretation has given both religious and irreligious people a spurious rationalization for a retreat from social action. Accordingly, the American temper has often been deeply anti-political, dismissing politics as necessarily corrupt. It is as the American temper has lost its theological basis and has thus failed to understand power as limitation as well as freedom that it has retreated from political action. But the retreat does not give us freedom from power. Candide could not even cultivate his garden without exercising freedom, human power. The power to reject or disregard power is itself an expression of power as human freedom and necessity.`

The idea of power is in no way alien to religion. Religion cannot be adequately described without one's employing the conception of power; likewise, power cannot be properly described without one's employing religious concepts. Power is both the basic category of being and the basic category of social action. The crucial question for both religion and social action is the question concerning the nature and interrelation of divine power and human powers. All social action is therefore explicitly or implicitly grounded in a theology, and all theology implies a fundamental conception of social action. Politics, therefore, must consider the theology of power as much as theology must consider the politics of power. When power is not considered in its proper theological character but only in its political, it becomes demonic or empty, separate from its end. Here power in the end achieves little but its own creation and destruction, and thus virtually denies itself as creative. In the human "order" this is what the Bible calls hardness of heart. The creative element of power is divine. The destructive element of power appears wherever power is divorced from an understanding of its source in the divine.

Definitions of Power

Having conceived of power as human freedom under God's law and love, we must now consider the varieties of our experience of power. We must turn to an examination of the relations between the two ultimate poles of power.

"All power is of one kind," says Emerson, "a sharing in the nature of the world." We may take this to mean that all power is capacity or ability possessed or exercised within the context of existence as it is "given." One is reminded here of Plato's laconic remark, "And I hold that the definition of being is simply power." Plato understands power as creative, as the condition and limit of humanity's social existence. For Plato this definition considers power as primarily law; it is transmuted in the Stoic and the Christian tradition as God's law, *logos*. Here power is not understood differently from what is stressed in the typical modern generic definition, wherein it is simply the capacity to exercise influence. The modern definition is true so far as it goes. But it is true only with respect to the power of freedom, the power to influence others, the power to control one's own behavior (freedom). Plato observes in the *Sophist* that power is present equally in the capacity *to be influenced*. Power exhibits duality, but it is one in this duality: There is no adequate conception of power as freedom except as it is simultaneously conceived of as law and except as it is viewed in a context of interaction ultimately grounded in the divine power of being (with its possibilities in terms of free and also ambiguous response).

God is not to be understood merely as a rigid law-giver, nor the human being merely in terms of freedom. As there is a dialectic between the two primary terms of power—human freedom and divine law—there is also a dialectic within each term. Plato suggests that power is twofold: it is both active and passive. In the Christian view the active and passive powers, in both God and the human being, are dialectically related. God is creative, redemptive power, active power. But God takes satisfaction in humanity's free obedience; in this respect God is influenced by human behavior. People possess creative freedom to influence themselves and others; this is active power. But people are also influenced by participating in God's power, that is, by being affected by God's law and love and by other people's behavior. This is passive power. Where mutuality of influence appears, both active and passive power operate; and, ideally, coercive power is employed primarily for the maintenance of mutuality.

This dialectic of power is sometimes overlooked by the definitions employed by the sociologists. The typical sociological definition of power as the capacity to influence the behavior of others in accord with one's own intentions, is a truncated definition. It refers only to active power. Max Weber's definition, for example, makes explicit reference only to this active type of power. "Power," he says, "is the probability that one actor within a social relationship will be in a position to carry out his own will despite resistance, regardless of the basis on which this probability rests." This definition makes room for force (influence by physical manipulation or threat), for domination (influence by making explicit what is commanded or requested), and for manipulation (influence that is effected without making explicit what is wanted, as for example certain types of propaganda). But Weber's definition does not explicitly include "passive powers," the capacities possessed by those who yield to one or another kind of active influence. Chester I. Bernard's discussion of communication in his *The Functions of the Executive* is at least more comprehensive in this respect, for he interprets executive power as requiring two-way communication, that is, as requiring the yielding to influence as well as the exercise of influence.

A distinction that cuts across the distinction between active and passive powers should be noted here. We may speak of "power of" as ability (for example, the ability to learn or the ability to express oneself) and of "power over" as the capacity to dominate. In the social arena when "power over" increases in a group of people, "power of" diminishes among those who are dominated. When "power of" is possessed by the members of a group engaged in social action, they have power in the sense that they participate in the making of a group decision, though of course the decision itself may lead to the attempt to exercise "power over" another group.

In all of these definitions, it is emphasized, then, that power does not exist in *vacuo*; it exists in some relation in nature and in humanity, and between individual or groups of persons, or between the person and God, the limiting, creative, and redemptive power. As Locke observes, following Plato, "Power is twofold; as able to make, or able to receive, any change; the one may be called 'active,' and the other 'passive,' power. Thus power includes in it some kind of relation—a relation to action or change." Power is a relation and it must therefore always be stated in two terms: law and freedom. In the realm of individual psychology the two-term relation of power is readily evident. Perceiving, knowing, imagining, willing, and feeling, are expressions of freedom, the power to choose. But perception implies its object; otherwise, perception is itself the creator of its object. The object is thus the condition of perception, and necessary to it. Perception as an expression of freedom is united with the object as an expression of necessity or law. This interrelated, active and passive character of power must be taken into account in any discussion of human behavior. We turn now to a brief review of the development of the concept of power in the history of religion.

Divine Power in Primitive Religion

Explicit religion involves the belief that there are divine powers with which humanity must enter into relations for the maintenance or fulfillment of meaningful existence. (We must omit here the discussion of the question whether the divine power may properly be conceived to be a being alongside other beings.) There is no notion of God, even among primitive peoples, in which deity is not power, or does not have power.

One of the most widespread primitive conceptions of power (which may or may not be associated with deity) is the idea of Mana, a mysterious impersonal force which can be in anything and which makes that thing strikingly effective. Archbishop Söderblom has suggested that in its nature and working Mana may be compared to electricity; it is impersonal, it can flow from one thing to another, and it can do a variety of things. It is a holy power in things, animals, persons, magical incantations, and events. As Söderblom says, "Numerous phenomena which we understand to be essentially different are explained by primitive man to be the operation of Mana: poison, the power of healing, the power of nourishment in plants, the killing effect of weapons, the growth of plants, success, luck, unusual events, mysterious impressions, the effect of a word, the course of heavenly bodies, everything depends on Mana or rather is Mana" (*Das Werden des Gottesglaubens*, p. 88). Since Mana is sacred and is therefore considered to be dangerous, various taboos are established for protection against it.

Among humans this power may be inherited or acquired. In either case, the possession of this "electricity"—a primitive understanding of law—can become the basis of authority and deference. In this fashion it can determine certain of the principal social patterns and even the hierarchical social structure. In addition to being an active power (in the sense we have defined) Mana sometimes is conceived to be also passive. Among the Polynesians, for example, ritual is performed partially for the purpose of regenerating or increasing the power of the gods themselves, so that while the people depend upon the gods, they are also able to strengthen the gods by their own exertions. The gods will run down if the tribe does not recharge them. Here both gods and humans have the power "to do" and they may also be undone by the other. Both the gods and the humans may dominate the other or be dominated by the other. In any event, the power of Mana "as electricity" is neither law nor ethics as we understand those concepts. Mana can be captured by an individual, thus raising freedom above law.

The modern, civilized person would consider quite fantastic any proposal that the conception of Mana should serve as a basis for social action. Yet millions of modern people have quite seriously accepted as a basis for social action an idea that is not entirely removed in character from Mana, namely, the idea of "blood and soil." This idea serves as the basis for a "religion" that in effect considers biological and tribal-territorial powers to be divine and therefore decisive for social action. Aggressive nationalism and "lily-white" Americanism live on these powers. Arnold Toynbee has argued that Anglo-Saxon Protestantism assimilated this kind of religion to that of the chosen people, establishing a new Canaan in the Western hemisphere. Like the religion of Mana, this modern tribalism is not in a universal sense ethical; it is pseudo-ethical because it is a law unto itself, thus contradicting the meaning of law.

Prophetic Conceptions of Divine Power

For a Christian theology of social action the definitive conception of divine power is set forth in the New Testament—the conception of power (*dynamis*) as forgiving, healing love working toward the fulfillment of the divine purpose of history. The law of grace is sovereign. This conception is a far cry from the primitive idea of Mana and from the powers on which primitive or "civilized" tribalism lives. Between the primitive conceptions and the New Testament conception there stands more than a millennium of religious experience. This period of history is very familiar territory to the reader precisely because its ideas have been decisive for Judeo-Christian theologies of social action. Despite its familiarity, however, we may, perhaps with some warrant, view it in the light of our concern with a theology of power as the basis for a theology of social action.

Conceptions of divine power very similar to the idea of Mana as well as tribalist conceptions of divine power are to be found in early Hebraic thought. But the power in which the ethical prophets placed their trust was a different sort. Although this power was evident for them in miraculous event and in ecstatic (though not orgiastic) experience, it was a power that became peculiarly manifest in the corporate life of the People of God, a view of the divine which had its roots in an earlier deliverance from bondage and whose goal was a universal, ethical purpose. Here power is conceived of as the freedom of the Jews under the Law; they were chosen and they responded by choosing. All events are therefore both power as the freedom of the human being and power as the law and love of God.

This prophetic conception was not the result of merely abstract reflection. It appeared on the occasion of a power struggle, the struggle for domination undertaken by the military empires surrounding Israel. It was developed as a reaction to the military weakness of Israel in face of the overwhelming strength of the great powers. As Max Weber points out, "Except for the world politics of the great powers which threatened the Israelite homeland . . . the prophets could not have emerged" (*Gesammelte Aufsätze zur Religionssoziologie,* III, 282). In a previous interim of peace, the Palestinian "states" had appeared, and with them a sense of superiority in the Hebrews, a sense of pride in past achievement (freedom) under divine guidance (law), and a faith in a glorious future for the nation (freedom under God's law). The revival of oppression at the hands of the Mesopotamian and Egyptian empires raised the old mantic vision of the power of an ethical, national deity to the level of the international as well as the ethical. The prophets were "political theologians" concerned with the destiny and the ethical significance of the state; they viewed the power of God—law—as operating through social and political institutions and in international relations, the expression of human freedom. This is a conception of divine power which in its magnitude staggers the imagination; indeed, it is the conception which the pietist, typically preoccupied with the immediate relations between the individual soul and God, always has greatest difficulty in comprehending or in taking seriously. Yet the pietist, like anyone else, participates in the institutionalization of powers which society defines and redefines.

It is worthwhile to observe here, in passing, that the activity of the prophets was itself possible only because of a peculiar aspect of the social organization of the society in which they found themselves. The prophets could not have emerged had they not been able to appeal directly to the people. In this fact we may see implicit a principle of freedom which is indispensable for any Judeo-Christian theology of social action. The lines of political communication and activity were not held in monopoly by the monarchy. Unlike the "prophets" of surrounding countries, the Hebrew prophets were not an adjunct of the monarchy. Weber, in a slightly pejorative sense, calls them "demagogues." Within the social stratification of their society, they were able to be the spokespersons to and for the poor and the oppressed. In their tradition there was a separation between charismatic and traditional authority which left the way open for prophetic criticism. In other words, the freedom of the prophet presupposed a separation of powers which in a narrow way bears comparison to the modern ideal of freedom of the press. This separation of powers which permitted the liberty of prophecy was related to the fact that the covenant between God and the People was not through the monarch; the covenants between God and the People and between God and the royal house were parallel covenants, and both were subject to prophetic criticism. The divine kingship was limited by this separation of powers. The will of God could be discussed by the prophets without license from the government; it could even be expressed through the mouth of the prophet against the monarchy.

Viewing the overwhelming power of the great empires and exercising the liberty of prophesying, the prophets elevated Yahweh to the Lord of history. In the course of time they claimed that God uses the great powers (for example, "My servant Nebuchadnezzar"—political power) as instruments for the punishment, the purification, and the education of his chosen people; he was raised above the gods of the world powers; and, finally, he was said to be the one and only God.

The prophetic conception of the divine power was shaped, then, in the stress of power politics; conversely, the conception of power politics was shaped under the stress of a new vision of the divine power. To the degree that the conception of divine power changed its character, Israel reacted differently to subjugation, indeed transcended it, and found a new meaning in it. The divine power was not only ethicized. It was also interiorized; it was interpreted as operating in the most intimate aspects of psychic experience and of divine-human fellowship. Both God and the human being were now seen to be bound together not only in the realm of politics but also in the inner life. This remarkable interiorization of piety represents the translation of the conception of divine power into a new dimension: it represents also a deeper conception of the conjugation of the active and passive powers. These two aspects of the divine and the human powers, the ethical and the interior, are so important for a Christian theology of social action that they deserve a closer scrutiny.

Since the present brief essay aims primarily to be a constructive statement rather than a historical one, we shall not try to express the Hebrew prophetic outlook exclusively in its own vocabulary. Rather, we shall try to present it in a way that readily lends itself to an appreciation of its perennial relevance for a theology of power.

(1) The power that is worthy of confidence is the Creator of the world and humanity. This is a mythological formulation; in essence it means that existence is grounded in divine power—the power of being, in law—and is therefore a divinely given realm of meaning. Christian theology has succinctly expressed this basic presupposition of the doctrine of creation: *Esse est bonum qua esse*. Being as such is good; it is of God. Good is possible only within being. God offers the possibility of good. The doctrine of *Imago dei* is an application of this view to the doctrine of the human being. Humans in freedom participate in this divine law and creativity. Recasting this affirmation in terms of a theology of power, we may say that to exist is to possess, or to participate in, the divine power of be-

ing; it is to be the beneficiary of the divine power which is the ground of order and meaning.

This means that the prophetic view renounces any radical asceticism in face of the material order. It rejects the cynic's notion that all power is evil, a notion that represents an extrapolation from the view that political power is evil. For the prophetic view, this false notion would imply that the perfect God should be perfectly impotent. On the other hand, prophetism rejects not only the fallacy that being is evil; it rejects also the fallacy that existence is simply good. There is a possibility of good or evil in existence. Both possibilities can express themselves in human action. Prophetism therefore laid a burden of responsibility upon all people. Escape from action to contemplation was rejected as a mode of irresponsibility. Escape from the material for the sake of the spiritual, the renunciation of the finite for the sake of the infinite, constitute irresponsibility in face of the divine possibility and command. There is no freedom *from* the world that is not freedom *for* the world. Matter is not a demonic power; it is not the enemy of meaning. Sin does not derive from the fact that the human being participates in a material world but rather from disobedience to the divine demand for love and justice. The fulfillment of meaning is inextricably related to things earthy, to soul *and* body, for both soul and body are God's creatures. It does not appear in spite of or in protest against the earthy. The order of nature, in humanity as well as beyond, demands human care and love just as it receives God's care and love.

Yet, the Judeo-Christian doctrine of creation asserts also that the divine power is not to be identified with the world or with any part of it. It is never capsuled anywhere in the world, not in a "superior" race or nation, not in a religious tradition, not in religious ceremony, not even in the prophet's word. The attempt to capsule the divine power is the attempt to control and manipulate it, to become sovereign over it; the attempt is blasphemous. "Thou shalt have no other gods before me." Everything finite stands under the divine judgment. "Religion" itself stands under this judgment. The basic threat to "faith-ful" freedom is the threat of idolatry— giving to the creature that which belongs alone to the Creator. This view is the basis of prophetic criticism. Prophetic religion speaks out of a religious vision; it is not first and foremost a movement for social reform. But the vision issues not only in prophecy against idolatry; it lures toward positive obedience to and fulfillment of the divine law.

(2) The power that is worthy of confidence, the power that alone is reliable, has a world-historical purpose, the achievement of righteousness and fellowship through the loving obedience of its creatures. As an ethical, historical religion prophetism is not mystical in so far as mysticism is interpreted as a flight above the temporal world into timeless communion with eternity. For it, time is not the enemy, as it is in much of Hellenism; time is not the order of deterioration. It is the arena of fulfillment through law and freedom, though it is also

the arena of God's judgment. The divine purpose is manifest not in abstract, timeless entities but rather in historical events and patterns of events, in events and even in periods in the life of the people. Past events become necessity in the form of judgment where once they were only elements in the arena of freedom. On the other hand, they are interpreted as evidence of the faithfulness of God. In the past God had chosen Israel and made a covenant in order to carry out his purpose in a special way. He had delivered Israel from bondage and slavery. Freedom from bondage is the working of a divine power, freedom from domination. But it brings with it the demand for a new commitment. The divine power, the reliable power in history, forms men and women into universal, righteous world-community. Where true community is being formed, there the divine power is working. Indeed, this is a way in which we may identify the divine power. Prophetic religion is a historical religion not only in the sense that it is concerned with the struggle between good and evil in history but also in the sense that it looks toward the creation of historical community of memory and hope with respect to God's working in history. Toward this end, humans may be unfaithful, but God will be faithful.

(3) The power that is reliable in history places an obligation to righteousness upon the whole community of the faithful as a community, though to be sure the fulfillment is in God's own time. The response to the divine power is responsibility. The covenant of God is

with the community and the individual members of it; it imposes responsibility upon community and individual members of it; it imposes responsibility upon community and individual for the character of the community and especially for concern with the needy and the oppressed. Religious institutions, cultus, political and economic institutions must serve God's righteous purpose. There is no enclave that is exempt from his sovereignty.

(4) The power that is reliable and sovereign in history offers itself as the basis of a fellowship of *persons*. Before working on the visible, outer side of history it generates the inner side of history and community; it manifests itself in the responsive, creative, healing powers of justice and love, of tenderness, forgiveness, and mercy. These qualities are not merely human devices. They are the capacities and feelings that express the fullness of the divine power. The interrelatedness of persons is seen to involve these interior qualities. When the people do not exhibit tenderness, forgiveness, and mercy, they are in their freedom frustrating or perverting the divine power. Prophetism is not only a religion concerned with the divine power as it manifests itself in the outer events of history; it is also an interiorized religion of fellowship between God and humans and between humans under God. This feature of prophetism is conspicuous not only in the writings attributed to the prophets. Its literary precipitate appears also in the *Psalms*, the most intimate devotional literature of the

race. Thus the power of God is strikingly personal in contrast to the merely impersonal, "electric" power of Mana. It is a passive as well as an active power; and it looks toward the expression of "power of" and "power with" rather than of "power over" (domination). The significance of this emphasis can be appreciated if we consider another aspect of the problem of the theology of social action.

The theological bases of social action cannot properly offer a blueprint for social action. The attempt to make a blueprint and to give it a divine sanction always runs the danger of issuing in idolatrous legalism. Yet the relevance of any theology of social action can become clear only when one discerns the demands that it makes upon social action and organization. Right attitudes are never sufficient alone. They must find embodiment in social institutions. Indeed, one must say that one does not even understand the meaning of "right attitudes" or even of a theology until one recognizes their implications for social organization. If no particular demands ensue with respect to social organization, "right attitudes" can be a snare and a deception, a form of organized irrelevance.

Now, when we search in the prophetic writings for an explicit statement of the principles of justice and love on the basis of which one might devise a theory of social organization, we get a rather "dusty answer." As Ernst Troeltsch says, the prophets did not work out these principles. But this does not mean that they were vague and inexplicit in their specific demands. Taken altogether their specific demands for social change are extensive; the prophets cannot be accused of being other-worldly.

Just at this point Troeltsch makes a radical criticism of the prophets as social reformers, as promoters of social action. In effect, he argues that when they became specific they tended to become also irrelevant, for they were not very willing to grapple with the actualities of the new economic and political situation in which Israel found herself; they indulged a nostalgia for an irrecoverable past. Their demands were not practical for their times and, he argues, they are not practicable for any other society in so far as that society is urban or is becoming urban. Several, if not all, of the prophets idealized an old, simple, half-nomadic, agricultural, small businessman ethic; they opposed the bigness as well as the luxury of cities; they deplored the violent force of wars of empires, the precarious entangling alliances with foreign powers, the pomp and intrigue of the court, the loss of the simple, friendly justice administered by the elders, the impersonalism as well as the bribery of the courts of the princes, the officiousness of state functionaries, the oppression of officialdom, the law and usages and abuses that are characteristic of any urban economy. So far from being progressive radicals the prophets were reactionaries in the sense that they wanted to return to the good old days. To a large degree their "social program" was atavistic. As Troeltsch puts it, "The prophets are representatives of that Israelite mentality in which the old customs of the fathers stand in closest connection with the Yahweh cultus" (*Der Glaube und Ethos der hebraischen Propheten*).

Troeltsch appears to suggest that the anti-urbanism of the prophets renders their conceptions of social justice anachronistic already in their own time. But there is a sense in which precisely this aspect of prophetism is perennially relevant, especially in an urban economy. Stated in sociological language, the yearning of the prophets for the rural ways of the idealized past was a yearning for a society in which primary, affectional relations are dominant. In the urban economy where division of labor is elaborate and social mobility is required, the total personality is not brought into play in most social relations. Secondary relations, segmented impersonal relations, tend to predominate. A certain alienation reflected in the individual's feeling of isolation, homelessness, restlessness, and anxiety is the consequence. The sense of alienation is created by the lack of intimacy, the impersonalism, the multiplicity of norms, the atomizing of obligations, the loss of communal solidarity. All of these consequences follow from the loss of primary ties. Luxury alongside neglected abject poverty, concentration of economic power, exploitation, callousness, intrigue, produce alienation of person from person, of person from the covenanted community, of person from God; they pervert humanity and society; in short, they alienate the person from the community-forming power of God. Alienation can appear of course where primary ties are strong (divorce is not unknown); but in recommending the return to the past the prophets were trying to cope with a fundamental and characteristic problem of urban life. They were trying to correct the evils of mass society by the restoration of primary relations wherein fellowship, friendliness, intimacy, common responsibility could again prevail. They wanted the return of the power of mutuality as over against the power of domination. They saw that the power of God unto salvation can work only when humans are not treated as things. They would have understood the Marxist protest against the *Verdinglichung* ("thingification") of the human being. This term is perhaps as good a symbol as any that could be used to characterize the major consequence of the frustration of the power of God as understood by the prophets. At any rate, no word could better indicate the pressing relevance of the prophetic ethic for the dehumanized anonymity of contemporary mass human being. The prophetic ethic may be atavistic in its details. In its essence, however, it is an ethic that is especially pertinent in face of what John Stuart Mill called "the prices we pay for the benefits of civilization," the drying up of the sources of great virtues, "the decay of individual energy, the weakening of the influence of superior minds over the multitude, the growth of charlatanerie, and the diminished efficacy of public opinion as a restraining power" (Essay on "Civilization").

As against Troeltsch, we must say that the instinct of the prophets was sound. Taken together with the other aspects of their theology of social action which we have already noticed, their demand for the values, the powers that attach to intimacy of fellowship, is a perennially relevant demand to be made by every Christian theology of social action. Love and justice can prevail only where they are supported by the fellowship, the friendliness, the concern of each for all and of all for each, the sense of brotherly and sisterly responsibility, found in the community of primary relations. These qualities of psychic relatedness are at the same time the working of the grace of God and the medium through which the divine power grows into history like a seed that grows "of itself," for through them the active and the passive powers of sensitivity operate in mutuality.

Conceptions of the Divine Power in the New Testament

The reference to Jesus' figure about the seed (employed by Jesus in parables that have metaphysical as well as moral depth) assists us to observe the way in which he continued, extended, and deepened the prophetic conceptions of the community-forming power of God. In his conceptions of Love and Law he emphasized, as did the prophets, the divine yearning and initiative for intimacy of fellowship between God and the person and between persons. But, going beyond their eschatological hopes (which we have had to leave out of our explicit discussion), he stressed the idea that the Kingdom of God has already "broken in." Moreover, Jesus transformed the Old Covenant into a New Testament, implying a new basis and a new world mission. He envisaged a more intimate relation between himself (the spearhead and earnest of the Kingdom now breaking in) and his community than that between Moses and the prophets to the People of God. The God of Jesus also seeks out after the lost and the neglected. Besides, he presents himself as a new, tangible manifestation and medium of divine power. "Moses received and gave Torah; Jesus *was* Torah, together with the power to fulfill Torah" (W. M. Horton, "The Christian Community: Its Lord and Its Fellowship, *Interpretation*, IV [October 1950], 391).

We should notice here another important difference. In his conception of the Kingdom of God, Jesus shared with the prophets, as we have indicated, the desire for intimacy of fellowship. In many respects his mentality and that of his immediate disciples was similar to that of the prophets in the sense that it was conditioned by agrarian protest against urbanization. "The gospel," says F. C. Grant "is, in fact, the greatest agrarian protest in all history." But the prophets do not appear to have formed continuing intimate groups in which their theology of power, their theology of fellowship, could find application. The Christians *did* form a social organization in which the power of the spirit, the power of love, could find organizational embodiment. Moreover, in the conception of the Body of Christ they found a new ontological basis for the working of the divine power that was in Jesus, namely, the *koinonia*, a group living a common life with Jesus Christ as its head and informing power. Participation in a believing fellowship became the soil for the working of the divine power. Again, we observe that the divine and human powers were interpreted as both active and passive; moreover, the noncoercive aspects of power were greatly stressed. The New Testament ethic is an ethic of abundance.

As touching the question of the theological bases of social action, however, we must observe that Jesus gave his direct attention to person-to-person relations. He was not a political theologian. He and the primitive church showed little direct concern for economic and political problems and institutions as such, the problems having to do with impersonal relations. This attitude is to be explained mainly by his sense of urgency with respect to the imminent coming of the Kingdom in fulness and power. St. Paul, however, gave impetus to a conservative evaluation of political and other institutions. "The powers that be are ordained to God." "I have learned in whatsoever state I am, therewith to be content." Despite these attitudes, the early church exercised an increasingly transformative power in institutions, partially as a consequence of the fact that the church itself provided an opportunity to people who had previously been excluded from exercising significant social-political power to assume responsibility in the exercise of power, that is, in participating in the divine creative-redemptive power and thus making social decisions. But beyond this, it surely must be recognized that the canon of Christian social action does not close with the New Testament.

Power and Social Action in the Democratic Society

The attitude of responsibility appropriate for achieving consensus toward the end of shaping social policy in modern democratic society is better represented by the nineteenth-century British theologian, William Whewell: "Every citizen who thus possesses by law a share of political power, is one of the powers that be. Every Christian in such a situation may and ought to exert his constitutional rights, so far as they extend, both to preserve the State and the Law from all needless and hasty innovation, and to effect such improvements in both as time and circumstance require; using the light of Religion as well as of morality and polity, to determine what really is improvement" (*The Elements of Morality Including Polity*, New York, 1845, Sec. 651). Although the fellowship of the *koinonia* is perhaps possible only in the church itself, the vocation it places upon the Christian in the world must presuppose the ongoing attempt to make its conception of the divine power applicable outside the *koinonia* as well as within it, in the latent as well as the manifest church. The theological and ethical principles of Christian social action which are appropriate for the church are ultimately the criteria for judging and transforming society. The Christian looks for a society in which all people may be treated as persons potentially responsible to God's redemptive purpose for history. And in working for it, we must perforce use that kind of fellowship today called the voluntary association, where within the church and outside it consensus is formed and social action is undertaken.

But between St. Paul and William Whewell there stands a long period of development (including the Left Wing of the Reformation as a decisive period) almost comparable in significance to that which separates the period of belief in Mana from the prophetic period of discovery of the Lord of history. Yet, the general framework of ideas provided by Jewish and Christian prophetism, together with its demand for responsible, communal fellowship, represents the orientation for the theological bases of social action which is imperative for any Christian who undertakes to fulfill the divinely given responsibility to participate in social action toward the end of offering loving obedience to the divine power, the Lord of history and of the human soul. Christian obedience looks toward the kind of social action and the kind of society that can provide the soil out of which the creative, judging, healing power of God may like a seed grow of itself.

The Prophetic Covenant
and Social Concern

More than anyone else, Adams has placed the idea of covenant on the theological and social-ethical agenda of religious liberals. In this essay he relates the phenomenon of bonding, found everywhere in nature and society, to the biblical idea of a covenant. The covenant that God establishes with "the people of God" in the Bible shapes the understanding of right relationship among persons and social groups. Adams describes the diverse, interrelated meanings of "covenant" in Western thought. This essay was edited from Alice Blair Wesley's transcription of lectures that Adams gave at Meadville/Lombard Theological School in 1977.—GKB

There is no such thing as a completely isolated being. Human beings are in relationship, and bonding is a characteristic feature of this relationship. Bonding is the development of attachment, loyalty, affection. It generates the collectivities that function in history. In bonding, human beings develop a sense of the past and of the future and even a philosophy of history.

Bonding in Nature and History

There are varieties of bonding. The most familiar and perhaps biologically inevitable kind of bonding is familial. One cannot come into existence except through hetero-sexual activity. The fact that the most intense hatred as well as the most intense affection can appear within the family shows something of the ambiguity of bonding. Another kind of bonding which has been of interest in Western culture from ancient times is friendship. My professor of Greek at Harvard used to say that the paradoxical thing is that one should find much in ancient Greek literature on the idea of friendship, and yet it is practically impos-sible to find any examples of great friends.

Another kind of bonding is the type that the Nazis attempted to consolidate, namely the bonding of pig-ment. The Nazi ideology was based on *Blut und Boden*, blood and soil, a philosophy of nationalism and racial supremacy. But they had no monopoly on racism. One of the most disturbing chapters in Arnold Toynbee's *A Study of History* [London, 1936], deals with the birth of racism in Anglo-American culture. His thesis is that after the publication of the King James Version of the Scriptures one book after another picked up the Old Testament idea of the "the chosen people" and adapted it to the Brit-ish. It became a kind of biblical nerve for British imperial-ism and especially for the idea of white supremacy. Bonding of pigment has been a vital feature also in American cul-ture; it continually provides occasion for conflict and for new attempts at reconciliation—for attempts to transcend the accident of pigment and to achieve bonding in the name of something more universal.

A few years ago I discovered a letter from Karl Marx to one of his friends, complaining about his wife and daughter putting on their best Sunday-go-to-meeting clothes to go off to a Methodist chapel. He said, "I've tried to be tolerant with them, but I really had an outburst last Sunday. I said to those two ladies, 'If you are so much interested in religion, I suggest one Sunday you stay home and read the Old Testament prophets, and you'll see what it is!'" The kind of bonding you have in some forms of Marxism, which has so much changed the planet, could not have occurred in Western culture without the background of the prophets. Marxism presupposes prophetism.

To understand this tradition, I want to perpetrate some generalizations. George Lyman Kittredge, the Shakespeare scholar, used to say that the art of teaching is the art of telling a lie and then qualifying it. I'm going to tell some "lies" of oversimplification and then make qualifications.

Historical Religion

The Western religious outlook may be characterized as a historical point of view. In Judeo-Christianity since the Old Testament prophets, and even before, the center of attention is upon events in history. The historian Williston Walker, asking why Christianity triumphed in the early Mediterranean period, answered that it had an event to point to, namely Jesus Christ, the Incarnation. The other religions, he said, had myths and legends and nonhistorical figures. Jesus was a historical figure, a cardinal event that could be pointed to. A historical religion is oriented to events that happen in history, to processes that raise one above history, and not to an inward, narcissistic journey. Even when it is nonreligious—when the old myths have died and it is secularized—the Western outlook on life is not one that promotes a merely mystical transcending of history.

Western religion, then, is oriented to events in history. One has to understand existence in terms of events, their processes, their outcomes, their catastrophes. This means also that a historical form of religion sees history as being formed by groups. Individuals are not isolated, but enter into bondings in history. These bondings, as they affect history and maintain some kind of continuity in history, find institutional forms. So historical religion is ultimately one that sees history in terms of persons in groups and in institutions. The idea of the person achieving fulfillment without participation in groups, without relatedness and responsibility in the face of institutions, is a form of escape from history and away from authentic, historical religion.

Further, in a historical religion the sense of the past is important, because events, groups, and institutions become the occasions and the sources of achieving personal and social identity. Let me give an illustration.

I remember seeing Robert Sherwood's play, "Lincoln in Illinois," when it was first presented. At the climactic moments one could feel the entire audience identifying with Lincoln. Here was an interpretation of the past, highly idealized but also deeply meaningful, for in that event I felt a sense of group identity in terms of a meaningful past.

A historical religion is oriented also to the future; it is eschatological. It understands the meaning of life in terms of the pursuit of a goal, to be realized in the future, for groups and institutions. A historical religion, then, has a sense of the past and also of direction towards the future. It is in this sense that many people have said that Marx represents the old prophetic and Messianic idea of a drive toward the future. The meaning of history is going to be achieved by a fundamental change of institutions.

A further feature of historical religion is that history, with its events, groups, and institutions, is understood in terms of periods. That is, there is a sense that what is going on now has had a past, but the present also has its peculiarly unique features, and one's social responsibility must be related to those unique features of the present.

The classical writer on this subject is Ernst Troeltsch. He said there are two characteristic features of a historical point of view. First, it is concerned with events. It tries to give meaning and direction to events, which are unique. As Oscar Wilde said, "History does not repeat itself. Only historians repeat each other." But history is related to events within history merely in terms of individual persons as carriers of ideas, since persons exist in groups and in institutions.

Second, Troeltsch said that a theory of periodization is characteristic of the historical point of view. People seek to understand themselves by identifying and describing the unique features of the present and the unique problems and responsibilities that the present calls for. It is interesting to observe the awareness of historical uniqueness and of periods in American fundamentalism. I was reared on the *Scofield Reference Bible*, in which the footnotes organize history according to "dispensations" running from the Creation to the Last Judgment. By the time I was eleven years old, I could rehearse these dispensations—the whole organization of history in periods.

The first appearance of such a philosophy of history is to be found in the book of Judges. George Foote Moore, professor of Old Testament at Harvard a generation ago, made one of the great scholarly discoveries of the twentieth century. He pointed out that the same stories appear in the books of Judges and Joshua, but that in Judges the stories are lined up in periods. The writer has tried to understand what is happening to the people of Israel and works out three periods. First is a period of military conquest, with the assistance of Yahweh. Then comes a period of betrayal, marked by a lack of adherence to Yahweh's law and by consequent military defeat. Finally, there arises a judge, who brings a return to Yahweh and to military conquest.

To use a farmboy's metaphor, Moore's thesis is: If you take the book of Judges and put it through a wringer, what comes out in the old-fashioned washtub is a series of "tags," as he calls them—periods marked by faithfulness, unfaithfulness, and the coming of a judge. These tags come through again and again. We may note that a major source of Marxism's appeal has been its similar theory of periodization: the original rule of the aristocracy; the present rule of capitalism, fraught with contradictions; and the "messianic" rule of the proletariat, to come.

Origins of the Concept of Covenant

Human social existence requires the achievement of a means of communicating about social existence, a characteristic feature of which is the invention of concepts. Concepts do not come down from heaven; they have to be invented. The poets are the legislators of humanity, as Shelley asserted at the end of his "Defence of Poetry," in the sense that it is by poetic imagination that the great concepts that interpret human experience have been devised. To be sure, the earliest poets, such as those who invented the concept of covenant, are unknown to us.

You recall the story in Genesis about Yahweh's instructing Adam and Eve to name all the flora and fauna. In the history of Jewish thought "naming" is one of the great theological themes; human beings, to achieve self-understanding and communication, have to name things. So in his commandment to name things, God was commanding something absolutely indispensable if they were going to be human. The story is told that Adam and Eve did their best, working for some time naming all the flora and fauna. Finally they sat down in the shade of a tree, thinking with some satisfaction, "Well, we've done what he asked—we've named them all," when suddenly something came hopping through the grass which they hadn't seen before. "What's that?" asked Adam. "I've never seen that before." Eve, who was the creative figure, seeing this thing hopping around, said, "Ah, ha! It looks like a frog to me." She named it.

One of the great namings in the history of Western culture, and one that represents a major thread in biblical literature, is the concept of covenant. It is interesting to observe how this concept was invented and the implications of the initial occasion of its invention. As generally happens, theological discourse here picks up a concept from ordinary experience and gives it a new and expanded meaning. A concept that originally applies to one aspect of existence is reinterpreted to explain the whole of existence. We call this process the radicalizing of a concept.

The concept of covenant was taken from the political realm and applied to the theological realm. It was made the basis of understanding the relationship between humanity and God, of understanding the nature of ultimate reality in terms of bonding. A political metaphor, in contrast to a metaphor drawn from interpersonal existence—a personalistic metaphor—has the broadest applicability. It interprets the whole human existence; everybody is in the political order. In this case it becomes the key to understanding the life of a people.

The political background of the concept of the covenant was first worked out by the American scholar George Mendenhall [in *Law and Covenant in Israel and the Ancient Near East* (Pittsburgh, Pa., 1955)]. He studied scores of treaties between a sovereign and smaller jurisdictions from the ancient Near East, going back as far as the fourth millennium B.C.E., and found analogies between them and the idea of covenant in the Old Testament. He showed that there were six ingredients of most of these ancient treaties, or covenants, which long predated the children of Israel's leaving Egypt: (1) a preamble—a historical prologue describing the past that has led up to this moment; (2) stipulations with regard to the agreements between the sovereign and the smaller jurisdictions; (3) the provision that the agreement must be periodically read in public and (4) must be kept in a sacred shrine; (5) blessings invoked on those who loyally maintain the agreement and (6) curses on those who are not loyal to it. In the literature of the covenant in the Old Testament, Mendenhall then finds very specific illustrations of each element.

The Meaning of Covenant

We may say, then, that in the Old Testament concept of the covenant the meaning of life is found in the processes and the responsibilities of history, namely in maintaining an agreement that provides order and continuity in the society. The meaning of life is rooted in a sense of obligation. Now I want to offer a series of propositions, those "lies" that have to be qualified if they are to take account of human experience with full adequacy.

I. The concept of covenant in the Old Testament prophets is the covenant made at Sinai through Moses. The first characteristic of human collective existence is commitment, that is, making an agreement, a promise. Promising is a characteristic feature of meaningful human existence. Richard Cabot, in *The Meaning of Right and Wrong* [New York, 1933], argued that meaningful thought and life require making agreements; further, the growth of individuals or cultures is seen not only in their loyalty to but also in their improvement of past agreements, including those which persons make with themselves. Martin Buber speaks of humans as promise-making, promise-breaking, promise re-making creatures; the making of promises and commitments Buber sees as essential to human nature.

II. The meaning of life is found in the processes and responsibilities of groups and institutions. The entire people, in this covenant view, is responsible for the character of the society. This is one of the great insights in history, namely that one is related to the collective in such a way as to be responsible for the consequences of one's actions and for the consequences of collective action. Institutional and not merely individual behavior is an indispensable aspect of human existence.

III. We see the Old Testament prophets' repeated emphasis on the idea that fulfillment of the covenant requires concern for the weak and the deprived. This is one of the most remarkable things in the Old Testament, an idea that has reappeared recently in John Rawls's influential study, *A Theory of Justice* [Cambridge, Mass., 1971]. This third point is to be connected with the second: the collective is responsible for the character of the society. Responsibility for promoting mercy and justice, especially for the deprived, requires criticizing those who have power in the society.

IV. The covenant is for the individual as well as for the group. We see this especially in the liturgical Psalms, in which individual meditation, prayer, and commitment are prominent. But they are never separated from institutional responsibilities. It is remarkable that the idea should have developed that the interior life, the prayer life, entails collective and not only individual responsibility. But equally remarkable and puzzling is our capacity to forget this.

V. The biblical idea of covenant is what I call a covenant of being. That is, the Old Testament asserts that the people's covenant is a covenant with the essential character and intention of reality. It is not merely a covenant between human beings; it is a covenant between human beings in the face of reality. The fundamental demands and possibilities of reality are not created by humans but exist in its very nature. The understanding of reality is appropriate only when it is seen in terms of an ethical covenant. The covenant is with the creative, sustaining, commanding, judging, transforming Power. This is the ultimate theological orientation of the Old Testament idea of covenant.

VI. The covenant includes a rule of law. It recognizes that meaningful, collective existence involves a consensus and a commitment with regard to what is right. It is a legal covenant. The desire for justice can be fulfilled only through collective concern with law as the major agency of social control. But there is a second part to this proposition:

VII. It is not only a covenant based on adherence to law but also upon trust and affection. One maintains responsibility for the collective, not, finally, because it is the law, but because of love. The responsibility is motivated by affection. Thus the breaking of the covenant is not merely a violation in the sense of criminality but in the sense of breaking faithfulness, of violating the affection that was the ground and nerve of the covenant in the first place. It is through God's love, God's grace, that we receive the covenant.

VIII. The covenant was produced by a prophetic criticism and carried within it a continuing need for the freedom of critical dissent. Prophetic criticism is a radical form of dissent, pointing again and again to the faithlessness, the betrayal of the covenant, by "the children of Israel." Thus the prophetic outlook becomes the major thrust for self-criticism in the culture.

We might say that Socrates brought judgment in Greek culture through dialectic—by asking the Yes and No of tough questions. Prophetic criticism directs its questions to the sins of the collectivity. In his book on ancient Judaism, the sociologist of religion Max Weber said that the prophets were precursors of the modern free press. I would say it this way. Old Testament prophetism institutionalized dissent and criticism and thus initiated the separation of powers. The prophets said that the culture was not under the control of centralized power; viable culture requires the institutionalization of dissent—in other words, the freedom to criticize the powers that be.

Social Responsibility

The covenant of social responsibility, then, is one that is rooted in a historical conception of the meaning of human existence, and not merely in a conception of personal religion. Personal religion, though it may have its own uniqueness and insight, gains adequate meaning only in relationship to the larger context of existence. The concept of the covenant is one of the great conceptual inventions of our ancient forebears for defining identity. We achieve authentic identity through an understanding of history, of our place in institutions, and in the claim that this is precisely the essence of reality, of being itself or God. The divine power liberates humanity through this sense of social responsibility, of dissent and criticism. We have here a major form of bonding.

Please observe the contrast between the form and character of this bonding and that of Nazi bonding. Bonding in Nazism is rooted in elements of nature, namely in one's own blood and soil and territory. The intention of Nazi religion is to enforce that bonding, regardless of law or universal standards, and to suppress every kind of free criticism. Nazism is oriented to nature. The prophetic covenant is oriented to history—to the demands of history and the achievement of meaning in history through social responsibility. The orientation to nature is of course not excluded. To make such a futile attempt to exclude it would be to ignore the hand that feeds us. Today we are beginning to recognize the imperative demands of ecology, requiring an extension of covenant—leading us again to the covenant of being, requiring also a reconception of the political symbolism in the direction toward organic symbolism. In other words, these different symbols and perceptions confront the demand for "creative interchange."

Restricted Covenants

It is easy enough in a homiletic mood to speak of a covenant of strength and love. But in many a human group there are other kinds of covenant—"restricted cov-

236

enants." We are all too familiar with the restriction that aims to prevent "undesirable" races or classes "invading" the neighborhood.

Besides those covenants there has been and is an equally pervasive, restricted covenant—the male sexist restriction that has kept women in a subordinate status and role, except perhaps inside the family.

Lamentably, scriptural sanction (especially Pauline) has been appealed to. In the fundamentalist church of my youth, women by sacred command were required to be silent in church meeting, even though they were the hustlers who kept an eye on the budget. They, and not the men, were required to cover their heads in church or during prayer (at home). These are examples of pious male-domination, yet they are feeble examples in contrast to the discrimination practiced in the marketplace and, in large measure still, in politics. It is still inconceivable that today a woman could be president of the United States, although in Britain a woman has been prime minister for years. This is one of our forms of apartheid.

It is significant that well over a century ago American feminists recognized their derogated status to be analogous to that of blacks. Here the relation between gender identification and the body could not be ignored. But times have been a-changing. In wide circles the feminists in the United States have been crying protest, making their claims, and forming voluntary associations to support them. We must say that their literature and public actions have been in advance of what is called "liberation theology" (such as has been promoted in Central and South America).

But as with the restricted covenants imposed upon the blacks and the Hispanics these covenants imposed upon women are still widely pervasive, particularly in the economic sphere (with respect to executive authority and to salaries and wages). Like children, they are supposedly not entitled to adult monetary remuneration.

In short, a long pull will be required before our apartheid is overcome and before anything like equality is achieved for either blacks, Hispanics, or women. This dismal situation is even more readily evident if we consider the large number of women who in addition to working are obliged to keep the home-fires burning. All the more dismal is the situation for women who are single parents.

In our search for equality for women the emphasis might well shift to a recognition of the complementarity of man and woman as intended by the Creator (already expressed in Genesis). Respect for each other flows naturally from the Creator's original purpose and could affect the quality of sensitivity to values within our present culture. Such a shift could prove to be pregnant with possibilities for an enlightened equality.

Further Reading

Books by James Luther Adams

An Examined Faith: Social Context and Religious Commitment, edited and with an introduction by George K. Beach. Boston: Beacon Press, 1991.

Not Without Dust and Heat: A Memoir, with an introduction by Max L. Stackhouse and a tribute to James Luther Adams by George H. Williams. Chicago: Exploration Press, 1995.

On Being Human Religiously, edited and with an introduction by Max L. Stackhouse. Boston: Beacon Press, 1976.

Paul Tillich's Philosophy of Culture, Science, and Religion. New York: Harper and Row, 1965; Washington, D.C.: University Press of America, 1982.

The Prophethood of All Believers, edited and with an introduction by George K. Beach. Boston: Beacon Press, 1986.

Taking Time Seriously. Glencoe, IL: The Free Press, 1957.

Voluntary Associations: Socio-cultural Analyses and Theological Interpretation, edited by J. Ronald Engel. Chicago: Exploration Press, 1986.

Two collections of essays and sermons by James Luther Adams have been published in special issues of *The Unitarian Universalist Christian*, edited and with introductions by Herbert F. Vetter; the issues are Vol. 32, Nos. 1-2 (Spring/Summer 1977) and Vol. 48, Nos. 3-4 (Fall/Winter, 1993).

Videotapes (VHS) Featuring James Luther Adams

The Adams Tapes:

Volume I, "No Authority But From God" (28 minutes), Volume II, "Religion Under Hitler" (26 minutes); James Luther Adams and George H. Williams commenting on figures and events in Germany, with the original films taken by Dr. Adams in the 1930s. Produced by James Luther Adams Foundation, First and Second Church of Boston, Boston, Mass., 1990.

JLA at Home: A Conversation in Six Parts With James Luther Adams:

"The Education of a High School Drop-out," "You Can't Go There Alone!", "You Don't Have to Send Your Spies," "Voluntary Associations," "Fundamentalists, Liberals, and Evangelicals," and "This Has Been the Greatest Day of My Life" (1 3/4 hours). Produced by George K. Beach, The Unitarian Universalist Church of Arlington, Virginia, 1988.